# BEHOLD!

## The Funniest Funnies Ever!

(Emphatically NOT for Dummies!)

**By Dr. Ron Pataky**

Your pieces are pleasurable to read, your mind is nimble, and you have a fine touch for gentle paradox.

- ***William F. Buckley, Jr.***

Your work is hilarious, and at the same time delightfully literate. This is must reading for anyone who wishes to save on his or her psychiatry bill. Ron Pataky, I suspect you are a genius!

- ***Phyllis Diller***

I am comfortable in saying that your work, as a collection, is the most inventive and consistently funny work I've encountered to date! Your splendid use of meter and rhyme is near perfection.

- ***James Michener***

I don't believe I've ever seen this much original thinking, and so many fabulous turns of phrases, in a single manuscript!

- V***incent Price***

AuthorHouse™
1663 Liberty Drive
Bloomington, IN 47403
www.authorhouse.com
Phone: 1-800-839-8640



Published by AuthorHouse 7/17/2012

ISBN: 978-1-4772-2516-5 (sc)
ISBN: 978-1-4772-2515-8 (e)

Library of Congress Control Number: 2012911092



This book is printed on acid-free paper.

# LET'S JUST GET THIS SILLY THING OUT OF THE WAY!

Isadora Glickenspat
Was neither thin nor very fat
But loved to sit and marinate in sauce

She wasted time by doing that
Complained the elder Glickenspat
Who, after all, was Isadora's boss

The two went round till ground was found
(With Isadora stark ungowned)
On which to meet regarding daily soaking

Miss Isadora in the fray
FOR saucy soaking every day!
To which the Angry Elder screamed, "You're joking!"

An answer, then, was nowhere found
With Izzie soaking in the round
In sundry sauces brimming to the top

Midst mighty hue and raucous cry
And Angry Guy disgorging why
The practice stunk and surely then should stop

But Izzie sat 'neath pansied hat
Not saying this nor much of that
Her mentals closed and not about to bend

Since pages hence and words galore
Will never ever tell us more
Let's close it so this silly rhyme can end!

AMEN!

# NEWS FLASH!!!

## BREAKING NEWS!!
## From Your Station

# WHEW!-TV



# WAR IS DECLARED!!

## Plus Today's Ball Scores

Today's news is poor
THE WORLD'S DECLARED WAR!!
We'll have a brief update
At seven
Meanwhile our chore's
To bring you some scores
And there's much more on war
At eleven!!

**AND NOW THIS WORD**
**FROM ZEPPO'S PIZZA...**

# Descartes Before de Horse

"Cogito ergo sum," he said,
"I think, therefore I am"
And though Rene is long since dead
He's left us in a jam

Could "Cogito ergo cogito sum"
Possibly offer a key
For the lesser, simpler, dimmer minds
That dwell in folks like me?

Could one more "cogito" flush the chink
To clear the cerebral jam
As it then more correctly would render "I think...
And therefore I THINK that I am!"

In any event, I disagree
And can prove, I think, in a blink
That all who somehow happen to be
Do not necessarily think

I, for example, don't think at all
So if I were to buy this rot
Despite the fact that my life is a ball,
I guess HE would say I am not!

# From 16th Century "Ronald's Place"

To bed do not go
With a vixen in tow
'Tis wiser to give her a wallop
Much better you might
To sit up all night
Than to foul your recline
With a trollop

© 1597 – W. Shakespeere & Nephuse Ltd.

From:

Gentle Breezes through the Treeses

# Love Poem

by

## The Poet

I'm havin' only shivers
At this closin' of the day
And I do believe
My mood is turnin' blue

I don't at all remember
That you ever looked this good
But then again
I don't remember you

# ODE TO A FLEDGLING PHYSICIAN

All I can hear is plaster...

The brand new doctor sat forlorn
Mulling affairs of the day
He had misdiagnosed, it was said with scorn
In every conceivable way

And they heard him grieve
As he took his leave, to brood out by the cactus
"O, what a tangled web we weave
When at first we practice"

# If I Were Just More Certain It's Possible I'd Be Sure!

Ever seen me here before?
Ever seen my face?
Know my stupid golfing score?
My height, my weight, my race?

Ever even heard my name?
To know who I might be?
And IF it's so, your answer's 'No"
Then how d'ya know it's ME?

# PAPPY'S PORTFOLIO

## (Memo to Sol)



**James McNeill Whistler**
1834-1903

**Among my aims:**
**Don't pose for James**
**(My son is such a bother!)**
**To spark her life**
**Why not my wife?**
**Thank you,**

*Whistler's father*

# DEAR DIARY

Hunt and Gamble
Trek out west
Vacation sounded tempty
Till learned at dawn
When chips are gone
The buffalo is empty

# LOST!

SMALL

# Reward Offered



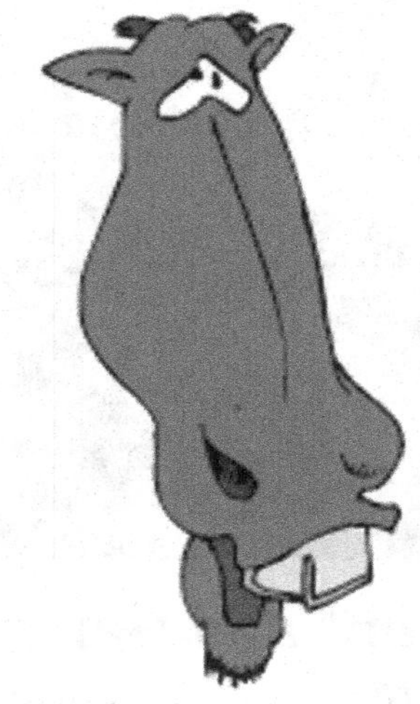

One eyed-horse
Coat burned and coarse
Despite the blast, still plucky
Has no left legs
But crawls (with pegs!)
Responds to name
Of "Lucky"

# It Ain't No Eiffel
# But No Trifle NEITHER!!

Seattle's Space Needle
Is quite an attraction
(Though next to the Eiffel
It's merely a fraction)

But one west coast farmer
(An excellent mulcher)
Has an idea, which
May aid agriculture

He wants to store grain there
Hoping the seed'll
One day be a haystack
That's found in a needle!

# Yeh Yeh ... And I Don't Have A Personal Zipcode Either!

The young man had dialed information
From one of those street corner phones
"Can you help me out?"
The fellow inquired
"I'm trying to reach Richard Jones"

"I'll need some more information," she sighed
"Do you have any street name at all?"
Perplexed for a moment
The young man replied
"Uh, most people just call me Paul"

# Getting Her Up To Speed On Her George Washington Trivia

"Roe versus Wade?
Was a choice that he made"
(For sure it's the answer
I'll give her)
"T'was the question he faced
As his boots were unlaced
Before crossing
The Delaware River!"

He diD it his
W
Ay

Meet DAnNy
DiNgaLinG
ThE CeLebRated
duNce

He nEveR

did ANYtHinG

tHe sAme wAY

oNce !

# Durn Boy!! Y'Ought'a Not Be Fiddlin' With The Girl!

Don't you fiddle with my daughter
Or I'll come a buggin' you!
I knew someone was fiddlin'
But I weren't certain who
It really don't a bother me
Ain't 'bout to blow my stack!
I don't object to fiddlin' some
But now she's fiddlin' back!

# Story of Adam and Eve Gives One Child A Good Ribbing!

The sermon that day
Was on Adam and Eve
And one little boy was astounded
The same little boy
Felt a bit of a peeve
As out of the chapel he bounded
Alone in his room
He poked at his ribs
Then he let out the gasp of his life
He yelled to his Mom
"I am NOT telling fibs!
I THINK I am having a wife!"

# When A Lanky Dude'll Come In Handy!

Say Cock-a-doodle-doo
Say Fiddle-doodle-doo
Say Yankee-doodle-doo
All quite zippy!
But if a gal's stayed
Many years an old maid
Then <u>**ANY**</u> dude'll do
**Bet your bippy!!**

# INDUCING THE POWER OF INDUCTIVE DEDUCTIVENESS

**REWARD!**

Sherlock Holmes and Dr. Watson have gone to the nearby waterfall region on a weekend camping trip. After a delicious, open fire-cooked meal, a final smoke, and a cup of steaming cocoa, they eventually slip into their plush sleeping bags and fall soundly asleep.

Some hours later, nearing three in the morning, Holmes awakens and hurriedly reaches over to shake his old friend. "Watson! Watson!" he whispers, "Quickly! Look up at the sky and tell me what you see"
Watson replies. "Good heavens, Sherlock, I see millions and millions and millions of stars!"

"What does that tell you?" continues Holmes.
Watson ponders for a minute. "Well, astronomically, it tells me that there are millions of galaxies and potentially billions and billions of planets.
"Astrologically, I observe that Pisces is hovering near Taurus.
"Chronologically, I deduce that the time is a shade or two past three in the morning.
"Theologically, I can see that God is all-powerful and all-present, and that we of humankind, on the other hand, are small and extraordinarily insignificant.
"Meteorologically, I do indeed suspect that we have a wonderfully clear and absolutely brilliant day to look forward to tomorrow. Why, Sherlock? What does it tell YOU?"

Holmes was silent for a minute then spoke.
"YOU IGNORANT TWIT …
SOMEONE HAS STOLEN OUR TENT!"

# CANNIBAL TABLE CHATTING

**"Frankly, I don't care much for your husband."**

**"Okay, okay … just eat the vegetables!"**

# BLIND DATE

OR

## "Bentley old chap, May I present Gwendolyn"

"Now Smile, no matter what you see!"

++++++++

"I feel the need to down one!
Again ... which eye is looking at me?"

++++++++

"I think that it's the brown one"

# Chalk This One Up For The Cow!

Bobo was a matador
He practiced on a cow
This made the cow exceeding sore
Who said: "The time is now!"

The cow approached him from the west
And opened all her spigots
Bobo took it in the chest
So much for pro-bull bigots!

# Whoa There, Uncle Pelican
# Why Not Just
# Sycamore & Millapot?

It's clear as a bell
Some are NOT hearing well
"YOU TWO! OVER THERE!
Are you DEAF, you??"

"While you're naming her twins
Will you wipe OFF those grins
Denise is just fine
But DENEPHEW?

# Attention Gang: A PELICAN Will Be Joining Us At Breakfast!

Diddle, diddle, dumpling
Our lad Will
Went to sleep
With a fish in his bill

We only KNEW it
When Ma said
"Willy-Boy's gone
That's a bird in his bed!"

# TOUGH LUCK, RANDY
# THEM'S THE BRAKES!

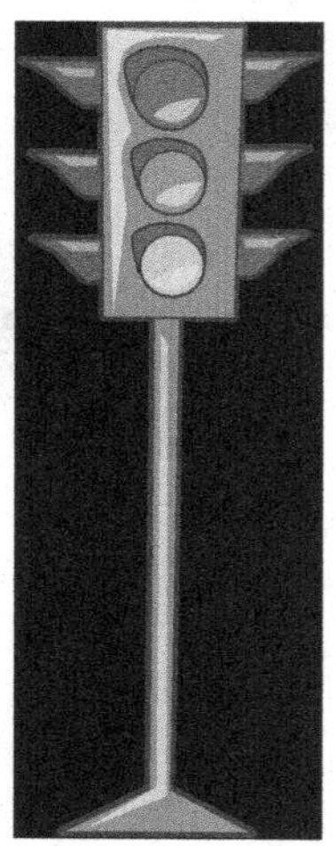

Randolph, the brown-nosed reindeer
(Who HAD been somewhat sickly)
Could run as fast as Rudolph
But couldn't stop as quickly!

## MORAL:

The herd that stops together stays apart!

# Pilot Says We Are Utterly Lost! But Making WONDERFUL Time!

"I don't have a clue
Just when we are due
Or whether to level or climb

"All the instruments say
We are lost (and should pray!)
Though we are making wonderful time!

"The compass has guessed
All directions are west
And flying this thing I'm bereft

"Of anything clear
As disaster comes near
(And I'm not even SURE that we left!")

# Hmmm ... You Say He Left With A Car & Returned Barefoot??

It weren't much, but it were OURS!

With "no gas" implied
Toad's car up and died
In front of that bar near the pass

So he strolled to the bar
And he traded the car
For twenty-two gallons of gas

But left with no bag
To carry his swag
Slim traded the gas for some booze

But the guy with the gas
Had to climb through the pass
So Slim sort'a gave him his shoes

# Recipes Come And Go But Beat THIS If You Can!

Chef Constantino prepares
his renowned "Bruised Omeletta Alfufu"

About the theme of gourmet fare
Fine chefs report the latest's
That the finest omelets anywhere
Are those whipped up by sadists!

# Strike Up The Music The Pigs Are In Gear!

(Ancient Greco-Roman Folk Refrain, Evil Curse, and Pig Dance)

When he first saw pigs dancing, Burt rubbed his sore eyes
But there they were ... prancing around in their sties
Wiping his glasses, he gazed down the lane
And he noted the grasses were new-wet with rain
Since he'd never before seen his future hams dancing
He tested the water (t'was non-dance-enhancing)
But all the pigs sashayed and generally bubbled
With cart-wheels that frankly left Burt slightly troubled
T'was then he discovered that when the sun popped
Though a few clouds still hovered, the pig dancing stopped!
He mulled it and glowered as he made his rounds
(Cause each time it showered his porkers lost pounds)
So Burt said a prayer for some mental infusion
And marveled how quickly it reached resolution
The pigs, it was clear, would be leashed on a tether
To keep them from waltzing in inclement weather

# New Fashion Column Features Chauncey's Tips

My fashion tips
Will come in snips
But promised you are many

Tip # 1

Who possesses
Sixty dresses
Don't look good in any!

Kisses, Chauncey

# Single Incident Kept Bedizzened Artist Rattle-Bummed For Years

He continually beseeched his friend, Van Gogh, but it merely went in one ear and stayed there!

Toulouse-Lautrec
Sensed a terrible wreck
When a stormy night led
To a blunder

A gust blew his hat
Beneath a black cat
Which he'd SWORN
He would never
WALK UNDER!!

# Different Strokes For Otherwise Ordinary Folks

Some splurge on folly, while others horde cash
Some prefer hearth to a corporate bash
Some order truffles, while some relish hash
Some of us ration while others act rash
Some crave a pager, and some are unlisted
And some are just happy to dial unassisted

# My Shrink Told Me To Get Back In Touch With Myself!

C: 2011 – Dr. Ron Pataky ---- Custom-Ransom-Notes.com

I wrote myself a letter
And just you wait and see
I'm going to feel much better
The day I hear from me

It isn't that I worry
But I'll tell you going in
It's good to know from time to time
Just how the heck I've been!

ONE SUGGESTION

# Have a Yearly Open Season To Annually Thin the Herd

If you're raising
A lawyer
Know this or take blame
Near a hundred per cent
Give the rest
A bad name

# IT'S SLIGHTLY TO MEDIUM RARE TO SEE IT WELL DONE!

If already ignored, please disregard this notice!

Many employees
Have not as yet done so
And boss-guy is having a cow!

We urge you to run so
When asked if you've done so
The answer's
"I'm doing so now!"

# With His Durable Grin They Decided To Use Him As A "Welcome" Mat!

There was little to say
On that unhappy day
When a steamroller ran over Marty

In their house was his wife
The light of his life
Making plans (they were going to a party)

Marty's hair they did comb
E're they cart-wheeled him home
(So to look like old Marty before)

But his wife at that hour
Was taking a shower
So they slid Marty under the door

# NO MILK TODAY, SLICKEROO... (BUT HER PRESSURE'S TIP-TOP!)

A slicker from the city
Saw a farmer 'neath a cow
With a bucket
On the gentle green of Cheshire
He asked him, "Are you milking??"
And the farmer grinned, "Not now...
TWICE a day
I like to check her pressure!!"

# At Home, They Were Much Like Any Other American Family!



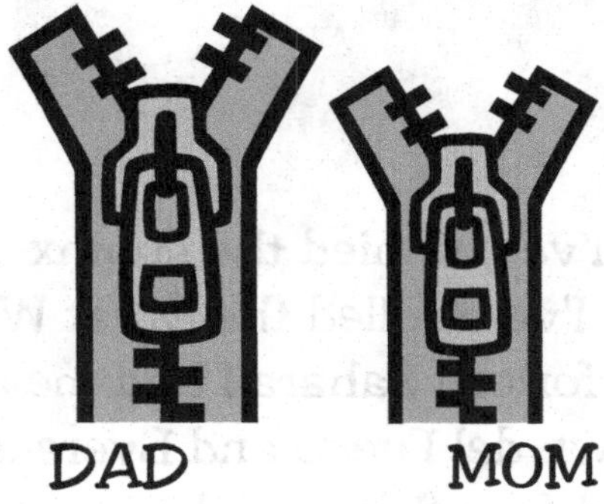

DAD MOM

A boy-zipper married a girl-same
And the girl-same in time changed her name
Wee zippers, of course
They would add to the force
And were happy as heck when they came!

They lived in a warm zipper cottage
Where they'd champion each new zipper cause
But troubles for sure
Seemed to always occur
When they'd visit the zipper-in-laws!

ON UN-RETIRING AFTER ALL

# All Thanks To Gorgeous Photos I AM Coming Out of Retirement!

I've shinnied the sphinx
And I've strolled the Great Wall,
In the forlorn Sahara I had me a ball
I've known del Fuego and Everest's chill
I've suffered four floods and a hurricane's will

I've swum the Pacific and fought bulls in Spain
I've suffered in silence and screamed out in pain
I've mapped Madagascar and dived with Cousteau
I've flown o'er the Pole and Victoria's flow

And while nearly all went according to plan
It was finally (last fall) when I fell on my can
So I've given up trav'ling in favor of scrounging
(Interpret that please as libation while lounging)

But then came the change
(Oh, those photos of Rushmore!)
And starting this moment
I'm traveling mush more!

# VOLUNTEER NEWS

## SEN. BOOBER'S STAFF BOASTS 'VOLUNTEER OF YEAR'

When office-mates noted
The verve of her lick
Giselle's stamps were voted
Most likely to stick

# A Further Possible Clue: The Sign Is Stamped: "Made In Occupied Bulgaria"

Searching for life as we probe our expanse
Can weary a man (if he gives it a chance)
This thing of creation, so deep, dark and still...
One can't help but ponder what's over the hill

But the chances of other life (much like our own?)
Get slimmer and slimmer as new probes are sown
One scientist reckons when all's said and done
That the gamble is roughly a zillion to one

So how do we deal with this most recent case?
(Just received back from a camera in space)
There on a red slope 'gainst millions of stars
Is a signpost that clearly reads: "Welcome to Mars"

# He Hopes Sound Reasoning Will Soothe Recalcitrant Wife

Don't fear, my dear
Your hubby's here
Let's <u>try</u> to
Get along
I'd like, it's true
To side with you
But then we'd <u>both</u>
Be wrong!

# WIFE WARNS HUBBY: BEWARE OF WRONG-WAY DOOFUS!

She called him to say
To be careful that day
As a madman was loose
On the highway

"He's speeding, they say
Down the pike the wrong way
In a dangerous, macho-type
Guy way

"So watch for that car
If you're going very far
I tell you the TV is buzzin'!"

"It's ONE car, they say?
ONE the wrong way?
I TELL YOU
THERE MUST BE A DOZEN!"

RELIGION PAGE

# "Hi! We're Here to See You ... But Doggoned If We Know Why!"

Agnostics go
Into a store
To buy a suit and tie
And then they knock
From door to door
But they're not certain why!

# By Then The Pathetic Doofus Needed A THIRD Opinion!!

The doc said it behooved
That Bill's lungs should be removed
A pronouncement that exploded
From the blue
Bill pleaded to Doc's minion
"Could I get ONE MORE opinion?"
And the nurse replied,
"OK ... You're UGLY, too!!"

# TO NOT TO BE OR BE?

**From a 14th Century collection attributed to one "Will, the Lysdexic," Udnersheriff fo Hammingnot**



# THINGS I HATE!

A real stupid riddle, trousers with cuffs
A "chat" while I piddle, encounters with toughs
Walks that are icy, sopranos off-key
Heads that are licey, a bad storm at sea
Foul-smelling meats and bosses who shout
A player who cheats and females who pout
Sillies who dip-dye their hair to hide age
Those pains in the butt who cannot control rage
Cars that are junkers or cars stained by sap
The "hair-dos" of punkers, the "music" of rap
Folks who like "pets" they can keep in a cage
Patrons who only like ham on a stage
Laughter in church, a "domestic" next door
A scared-to-death puppy or bleach on the floor
What some call "correctness," near-all "modern art"
Germs that infect us, a wobbly old cart
A down-trodden bum who's disheveled and plastered
A poor filthy slum that is owned by some bastard
And then there's a beggar (who's been there a while)
And the "generous" someone who gives him a smile

I've decided at last just to forego this race
To move on ahead, and to go at my pace
On the whole, with a frown, and until these things cease

**I would rather be naked
and nibbled by geese!**

# Polyester & Watercress Don't Seem To Do That Well, Either!

Baa, baa, black sheep
Have you any wool?
Yes sir, yes sir
A dozen bags full

Some becomes clothing
And some of it don't
But ALL of it grows
Where cotton just won't!!

# Who Will <u>EVER</u> Forget The Blizzard of Aught-9?

The chill was intense
The wind numbed the sense
So cold that the horse
Wouldn't pull!
Freezing our souls
We shivered in holes
And we ate our sheep
Just for the wool!

Tornados come in funnel form, in weather that is
usually warm, preceded by a sky that's gray,
unless, of course, it's night, not day, in
which case there's no clue at all, of possible impending squall, except perhaps
(which you won't see) a now-and-then
uprooted tree, or barns that move
with quite a clatter, several
fields before they shatter, im-
bedding with a mighty breeze
tiny shards in full-grown
trees, by which time a
prudent feller hastens
to the nearest cellar,
(or-din-nar-ly can
be found somewhere
nearby underground)
there to quake 'til
by-and-by, his house
is sucked into the
sky, leaving him
and wife as able,
praying 'neath a
basement table,
to get, despite
their lingering
fright, some
sleep before
the morning
light, mind-
ful as they
hit the
hay to-
morrow
is an-
oth-
er
day......

## A Primer on Tornados

# Worse Even Than the Night He Called the Tribal Chieftain A Bingabong!

He scraped with his bevel
To Pleistocene Level
And found
The consistency porous
He thought it would last
But he exited fast
When he butt-nicked
A small brontosaurus!

# C'Mon, Gal!

# For 32 Cents A Gallon It Weren't All THAT Bad!

A pretty bad beer labeled 'BUMP'
Was drawn from a gasoline pump
Said a guy in a car
As he drove to the 'bar'
"Will you please put a head
On my BUMP"

# Illustrating the Ongoing Exasperating Diabolism Of Bag Tag Lag

I said to the clerk at TWA
"I am flying one-way out to old Santa Fe
I've special instructions, replete with the tags
On how I would like you to handle my bags

"The first should be sent to the airport in Dallas
The next one direct to the famed Caesar's Palace
Please forward the third to Atlanta's fine fleet
And that then will render my journey complete"

----

"Oh, we can't do that sir,"
She said with a sigh
"That simply is <u>NOT</u> how bags flow"
"And why on earth not?"
Came forth my reply
"YOU DID IT A FEW WEEKS AGO!!"

# And our Jerseys Were Dark Red (So Splatter Wouldn't Show!)

Football?
In high school?
This might be a clue

School colors
At my school
Were plain black and blue

# Should He Maybe Take That As a "No" Then?

Bragged the boy turtle-dove
Out one night turtle-dovin'
"Some bird tonight's
Gonna get her some lovin'

"Hoo," said the owl
Sounding not all that wise
"You can bet your night goggles
Tain't YOU, Banjo Eyes!

# EGAD! Surrounded ...
# By Beauty And The Bucks!!

We learn very young
That girls involve "duty"
(Like lending our coats in the frost)

A girl, we learn quickly's
A body of beauty
Entirely surrounded by cost

# Just Another Ho-Hum Day At the CIA

C: 2011 – Dr. Ron Pataky --- Custom-Ransom-Notes.com

Tap softly, please, whenever you're ready
Since taking that bullet, I'm still not too steady
And then only whisper of what we've conspired
My hunch is that lunch <u>and</u> the transom are wired!

I've usually felt safe here with only insiders
But I'm seeing more of those virulent spiders
And only t'was <u>after</u> I gouged out her eyes
That the maid spilled the presence of dozens of spies!

One in particular (part of her tattle)
Has slipped in my sock drawer a snake with a rattle
Another, a huge chap with black, hairy chest
Has introduced anthrax to my tube of Crest

Still another, a female, has come on in spades
By slathering tetanus on my razor blades
And finally, this mug with a gaping red scar
Has rendered quite useless the brakes of my car

Yeah, some call 'em risky, these days full of fears
And to some it's not really...well, much of a life
Till I simply point out that it means thirty years
That I <u>don't</u> have to waste hanging out with my wife!

BULLETIN

# New Product on Market Excites American Moms



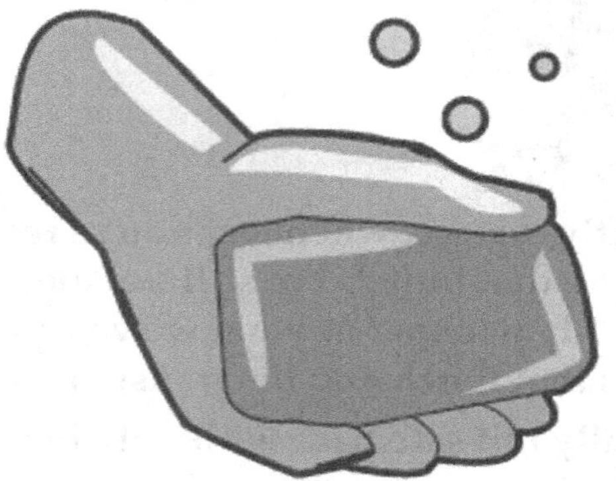

Mothers have hope
From a thing they call "Soap"
As long as instructions
Are heeded
One dose a day
Keeps tarnish away
And you simply repeat it
As needed

# And, Please, Please
# Make It on My 100th Birthday!

When I die, and hope it's at my beach house in Tahiti
And at the bier, she'll shed a tear,
my jasmine-scented sweetie

And when I go she'll have to bear
Games without her playmate there

She'll wipe her eyes, and choke back tears
(You know, of course, it's been two years)

Days of joy and evenings dear
Frisky bliss throughout the year
And don't forget the nights and such
Gone for good a lover's touch

Postponing, then, her quest for knowledge
GRIEF IS SUCH SHE MUST QUIT COLLEGE!

POSTSCRIPT

One more thing would drive her wild
If, after all, she was with child
And surely, then, the final bomb
SHE'D HAVE TO MISS THE SENIOR PROM!

# *As Translated From The Original Ancient Farcical

C: 2011 – Dr. Ron Pataky --- Custom-Ransom-Notes.com

If thee would
A name that's good
And fain would keep alive it
Do thy good
In public-hood
And all thy filth in private

# It's Not <u>Like</u> Droppin' In For a Bloody Marian!

C: 2011 – Dr. Ron Pataky ---- Custom-Ransom-Notes.com

Young Fangston
Shed his cape and hair
And said
"Just let me think"
There's blood, blood
Everywhere
And not a drop to drink

# The Special Gift That Keeps Him Guzzling!

Give him a fish
And he eats for a day
And then the last morsel
Is gone!
But TEACH him to fish
And you give him a way
Of guzzling beer
Until dawn!

# And Make DAMNED Sure The Soil Is Grounded!

Storms are predicted
With chaos inflicted
And resources bound
to be tapped
The thunder, it's said
Will awaken the dead
So make <u>certain</u>
they're properly wrapped!

HERB'S TIPS FOR A NEW DECADE

# Assessment Methodology

Assessment centers
Line the halls
You step up where they guess you
But lacking charts
You flow to stalls
Wherein they more or less you
You stand around
('Tis quite a mess)
Till most are ache-ly sore
Until they find
That some are less
While quite a few are more!

# 'Bottomly' Named Absolute Tops Among Quality Cadavers

Ichabod Rumpo - Salesman of the Year

**JINGLE**

**To the tune of:**
**"TAKE OUT YOUR FALSE TEETH, DADDY**
**MOMMA WANTS TO SCRATCH YOUR GUMS"**

Bottomly Cadavers
For the best there is in flesh
Nicely oiled
Never spoiled
And always packaged fresh

In flags or bags (no tears nor snags!)
We ship throughout the world
In town or glen
It's priceless when
A Bottomly's unfurled!

# Observed One Observant Observer: "Most Bumps Don't Have Ears And A Nose"

Starlings would peck
At the bump on his neck
(T'was benign, though it kept him in bed)
Explained Dr. Gump
As he fondled the bump
"We are thinking the bump is a head!"

BLOW OUT SALE!

# New Car Starts At $51,300
# As Shown: $149,750

"It starts at a number
That will not encumber
It's one of our
ONCE-A-YEAR deals!
Price starts in the fifties
And then you add nifties
Like windows and engine
And wheels!"

# AND ... She's NOW Talkin' About Cookies For Santa Claus!

## There's just no end to it all!

May as well wash up 'n get started!

My chores more and more
Are becoming a chore
And it's MORE of the chores
That I fear!

Like rinsing my socks
And RE-setting the clocks!
And **BOTH** of them
Two times a year!!

# Wild, Isn't It, What A Little Bronze Padding Can Do?

A mannequin fell for a statue
Whose figure was simply sublime
And although the statue continued aloof
He imagined he'd win her in time
When he then struck a pose to be kissed
She growled NO! ... and the guy wondered why
"Don't come another step closer," she hissed

"UNDER THIS BRONZE I'M A GUY!"

# SOMEWHERE NEARBY ...
# THEY'RE NOW WORKING
# ON A SUITCASE CHILIBOMB!!

The Chili Cook-Off would settle the matter
T'was Ichabod's chili or mine
My wife had the wisdom to bet on the latter
The plan was to win and then dine

Ichabod's chili proved naught but a joke
No question my chili was greater
It sat near the judges, and YOU saw the smoke!
And we all later dined at the crater!

# Chronic Drooling Overcome With Help Of Common Household Item

Like the song says, Boobie

**"Blotters are a girl's best friend!"**

When chronic drips
Escaped her lips
We knew she wasn't fooling

The doctor trips
Brought many tips
About her chronic drooling

The drip went on
From dusk till dawn
And also plagued her daughters

Till testing showed
The dripping slowed
When sucking flavored blotters

# Church Bulletin

Near all of our ladies
Have cast-off clothing
Please go to the hall
Where we'll seat you

Go left through the gables
Their clothes are on tables
And all are quite anxious
To greet you

# Quoting One Critic: "Less 'Podge' Might'a Whipped De Whoozies"

With artfulness, Dodge
Painted Hodge upon Podge
To shift his career into kickin'
But the canvas he'd splash
(In the end simply rash!)
Was to hastily whoozen and sicken!

RE-TOLD BY A DAME IN A BAR

# He Told Me That Nuclear Fission Requires Special Gear!

Nuclear Fission
Was his field
And marked thus
On his crate

He was asked
By a dame
Who'd learned his name
"So ... what do you use
For bait?"

# Sires! Just think
# Of the Whooshy
# We're Going To Save!

There were two ancient windmills
Of which it was decreed
One must be destroyed

(And I quoth)

"Tis a right sinful waste
Of most valuable wind
To continue the running of both!"

# Eventual Goal Is Huge Semi-Rectangular Island

Just south of Pitcairn, a mere stone's throw
From Krakatoa

He had four valises
All packed full of dirt
Plus a bucketful in his bandana
He confessed over wine
At the Idaho line
"I am gradually stealing Montana!"

Clock Strikes Mouse!

# Indigent Rodent Is Victim Of Overnight Hit & Run

**Witnesses Say Guilty Timepiece Just Kept Going!**

Near-victim describes close call

Hickory Dickory Dock
TWO mice ran up the clock
The clock struck one
And his life was done
The other, merely creased
Was treated and released

# Descartes Before de Altar!

Philosophers
While still in my teens
Occasionally made me tingle
"Cogito ergo solo" means
"I THINK
THEREFORE I'M SINGLE!"

# Congressional Buffoons Stick It To Voters Yet One More Time!

C: 2011 - Dr. Ron Pataky ---- Custom-Ransom-Notes.com

United States Congress unveils
"OFFICIAL HORSE"

Congress chose
To make a horse
(By vote their favorite mammal)
But had
(When things had run their course)
A cute but gimpy camel

# Decent Compensation
# (When You Think About It!)

Place One Single Place Place Two

Two places at once
I never can be
A discovery that's not all that nice
Until I remember
The thousands of times
That I've been in a SINGLE place twice

# Adult ADD: It's Often Manifested as

One problem we see
With adult ADD
Is a terrible struggle
To focus

Yet ANOTHER we see
With adult ADD
Is a terrible struggle
To focus

A poem concerning the various possibilities,
and the possible impossibilities as well,
of determining the best way
to divest your canine and feline friends
of the horrendous curse
of various bugs and/or mites that
may or may not inhabit
homes, barns, and other places
in your area!

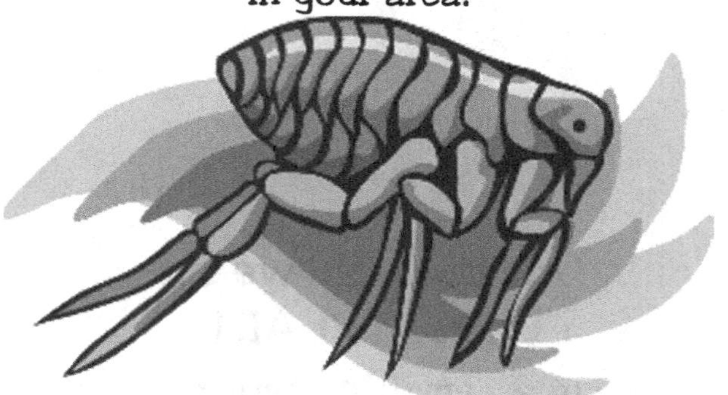

"Poems are made by fools like me
But only RAID can croak a flea!"

# One-Part Of A Notorious Russian Tragi-Poem

Daughter Kuklova says truth will out!

Eerie tales abound
Of the stout Czarina's tippling
With priceless boot
Whilst she was sodden, squozen

For remainder of poem
See 'Czarina'
Vol. 17 – p. 881

# The Kind You'd Like To Take Home to Phydeau

My latest blind date
Had a face like a grate
As I came face to face
With the truth
And if that weren't enough
Lengthy decades of snuff
Had severely discolored
HER TOOTH!

# And Her First FOUR Husbands Died Awful Funny, Too!

A germ grew tired
Of her mate
And so arranged his killin'
By lacing his morning
Garbage plate
With deadly penicillin!

# DEATH INSTRUCTIONS

**U. S. Government Stuff!**



When you know
It's time to go
Please don't be a bore

Tip-toe out
With ne'er a pout
And please
DON'T slam the door!

# Just Live Life As If
# It's All Just Temporary!

(Psssst ..... it is!)

... (NO!)

The "music" scene
Is bad today
(As every critic knows)
The tragic truth?
(Except for youth):
It will NOT decompose!

ON PHOTOGRAPHING THE CITY OF LIGHT

Dudley Fission: the current Toast of Paris Paris!!

# Paris Visitor Captures BOTH In Single Stunning Snapshot!

His name was Dudley Fission
And his constant double-vision
Would combobulate his Paris trip
For hours

Yet in spite of faulty eyes
He would grab the Photo Prize
For his
"Magic of the Awesome Eiffel Towers"

# She Glazed Over At The News; THEN Went Jelly Up!

There is something
About your tummy
And I feel compelled to note it
TODAY'S bad word
Is "DONUT" and
I WILL NOT sugar-coat it!!

# [Their Best Friends Included A Champion Boxer And His Husky Eskimo Wife]

"I shure do envy them two"
says neighbor Rufus

A Pointer and Setter
Felt none had it better
And knew that their love
Was anointed

Daily they'd gauge
The rewards of old age
But mostly they just sat
And pointed!

# In Short: Is A "Hole" A Presence Or An Absence?

It's one of my goals
This matter of "HOLES"
(I'm not sure the whole thing is fair!)
Does a hole into view
Mean that something is NEW?
Or that something is no longer there?
Let's face it, a hole
(Though it sounds rather droll)
May fool you until you come to it
You can beg and cajole
But you can't SEE a hole!
(What you're probably seeing
Is THROUGH IT!!)

# And This Is Not (It Appears) A Trial Separation!

The fact that I'm living
So high on the bone
In fact is only a start
My income and I
If the truth be known
Could be said to be living apart!

# Whew! Thank Heaven 9's ON TIME This Morning!

"How soon is nine o'clock?"
She gasped
(Her eyes were starkly wide)
She wore a crimped expression
As if sucking on a lime
"Only twenty minutes now,"
I soothingly replied
"And mercifully
It's running right on time"

# WITH MY PANTS NOW OK
# I'M WORKING ON MY GASPS

Whatever things may cause it
A skeleton in the closet
Is not a thing that I would like to chance
But there was dirty laundry
Occasioning a quandary
(And my lady, oh my goodness, how she rants!)
I've never seen her quicker
(She never touches liquor)
And closet bones did <u>NOT</u> my love enhance
But seeking to make use of them
I figured I'd produce of them
A couple dozen hangers for my pants

# Powdered Pee Explodes On U.S. Urinary Market

C: 2011 – Dr. Ron Pataky ---- Custom-Ransom-Notes.com

No more, the dangerous, inappropriate,
and highly illegal Lawn-Whiz!!

Finally we
Have powdered pee
Which means we won't outlast it

And you will <u>love</u>
The ridding of
Just find a wind and cast it!

And if you're led
To pee the bed
(Which blew parental trust)

Good-bye to pain
Of yellow stain
(Though powder may cause dust)

# Going Once, Going Twice
# Going Thrice, Going ... (Oh the hell with it!)

I'd been here before
Though I'd not a clue when
(The conundrum was not all that nice)
But damned if I'm not
Now back here again
And coping with déjà vu twice!

# Innovative Gimmick Colors Cheeks, Necks, Shoulders Of Area Young'ns!

Last Easter (it's true!)
To attempt something new
We placed several buckets
on kegs

And then all the guys
Filled the buckets with dyes
And we had the kids <u>BOB</u>
for the eggs!

# Consider:
# Man And Antibiotics Are The Interlopers!!

Disease had thrived
When man arrived!
No matter raves and rants

Deny the worst
But IT was first
So give disease a chance!

# Why Not FLY DOWN
# For Pete's Big Opening!!

PETE'S PLUMBING DRIVE-THRU
Is a notion that's new!
We have been here
Just over a week!
Why not zip it on down
To the best place in town
For CONVENIENTLY
Taking a leak!!

# They Were, However, Able To Retrieve His Batteries From the Steaming Gravy Depths!

His eightieth reunion
Was a sparse-attended thing
But he nonetheless was happy
He had come

He marveled at the fest
Grabbed a giant turkey breast
And he promptly bit off more
Than he could gum!

# All Right Already...! Better Maybe He Had Screamed <u>In</u> <u>a</u> <u>Mirror</u>?

A dyslexic rabbi
Much distraught
As a semi backed over his toe
Stifled a tear
For what seemed like a year
Before finally bellowing

# It Was Probably More Trouble Than It Was Worth!

He invented to cater
A huge elevator
With room in the foyer to sup
The ride was exquisite
A glorious visit
One thing: It would only go up!
It had every touch
(Though the view wasn't much)
With candles a touch from the past
But having no "down"
(In this case a noun)
Its first journey up was its last!

WHERE ARE THEY NOW?

# YOU'VE HEARD THE NAME A ZILLION TIMES; BUT WHO IS THIS GUY?

His name is known throughout the world
A man of saintly spheres
His, a world of dreams unfurled
Through many times and years

A vapor-ring of confidence
Shown 'round him like an arch
His wisdom helped to make some sense
Of life with too much starch

"THE HUSH OF LIFE IS WRAPPED IN HUGS"
[The quote that brought him fame]
And that is how ENAMEL GLUGS
Became a household name!!

# Even Terminal ILLNESSES Can Wrench Things Up!



**END DEATH NOW!**

JUST SAY NO!

Expiration
Slows the nation
Messing up our gauges
By my account
THESE deaths amount
To millions in lost wages!

# If It's Marked "DOWN" My Wife'll Buy IT!

C: 2011 – Dr. Ron Pataky ---- Custom-Ransom-Notes.com

Under new management!

If it's marked down
My wife will buy it
(Sometimes I just hate 'er!)
When last in town
With <u>it</u> marked "down"
She bought an escalator!

# The Very Private Diary Of a Boy Scout

My right ear is deaf
From a westerly wind
And the sun often shines
In my mouth

And moss and ferns grow
On the back of my neck
'Cause I normally stand
Facing South!

# And Plus: ALWAYS Name A Designated Musher!

Eskimo man
For many suns
Teach two main things
To de little ones:
*Stay away
From de whale
When de big fellow blow
*And do not eat
De yellow snow!"

# It Was Later Discovered
# They Had Simply Overbooked!

(Several demanded to see the manager - INSTANTLY!)

All her life she was faithful
She glowed in a crowd
And she longed for the gates
They call "Pearlie"

But she joined the crowd
Sleeping out on a cloud
When they flew in
A couple days early!

# Well, It IS More Taxing Than Bird-Spotting

To spot a hundred leopards a year
In Kenya's considered quite rare
But that was the claim of Lord Rumsey
With the world and all sitting there

But one peer has called him a liar
Saying Rumsey can boast 'til he rots
"He can blow 'til he's blue,
But I'M telling you
That leopards are BORN with spots! "

# As Daydreams Come & Go
# This Baby was a Masterpiece!

Fantasy's best!
Like when I went west
Determined them crooks
Would be rattled!

I set the bums swimmin'
Seduced all the women
Called Black Bart "a shit"
Then skedaddled!

# As Proof, They Had Polaroids Of Rumpled Mayonnaise

Two feisty pickles
Had burgled some nickels
And here is the story they fed us!
They said they were sliced
At the time of the heist
And were lounging that night
on some lettuce!!

HOME-TOWN NEWSPAPER

# Loretta's Boy Ferd Getting High Marks On Oklahoma Farm!

Lookie here, Agnus ... story about Ferd!

His many offspring famed him
(The girls all called him Ferd)
And all the bull-ettes named him
The workhorse of the herd

A PAGE FROM THE SIXTIES!

# Stoned in a Field SOMEWHERE!

Larry, Larry, blond and hairy
Tell how your garden was
"Man, poppy seeds
And funny weeds
And sooner or later
FUZZ!"

# BEAUTY BOUTIQUE PUTS OUT CALL FOR SPARE SPATULAS, SCRAPERS

A cascading dowager
Braved the salon
And was told by Pierre (what a lout!)
"Your remarkable lack'll
Require some spackle
And here and there touches of grout"

# Feds Nix Exam Claims If Not Conducted In Proper Setting



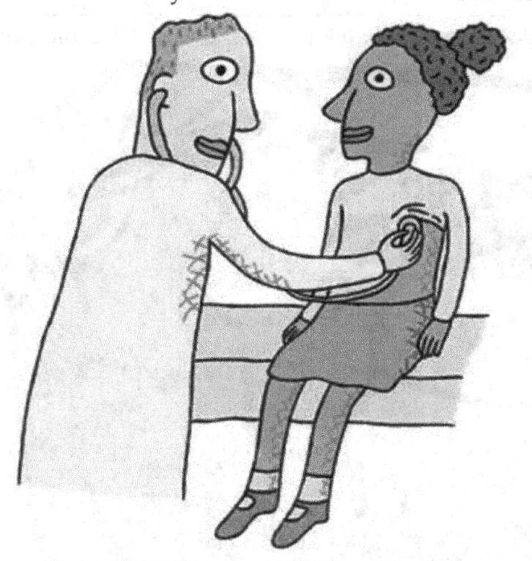

This is probably okay

Feds said today
Re: tricks and shams
And cons and stuff and looters
We will not pay
For BREAST exams
If carried out at Hooter's!

# HOWDY HORSE: According to Rumor A Decidedly Early Bloomer

He told them the great horse's handle was Howdy
A horse of un-horse-like contortions
The rumor went 'round until facts became cloudy
That Howdy had myth-like proportions

The rumors endured 'till the cowboys got rowdy
(And some would deny them, of course!)
Until they found out NEVER WAS, was this Howdy
But simply a name with no horse

# Wild Onions Along The Fence-Line Helped Enormously!

A little crispy side on the side
and whoopee doo, Mama!

Humpty Dumpty sat on a wall
Humpty-Dumpty had a great fall
All the king's horses
Stood munching their hay
While the king's hungry soldiers
Prepared a soufflé

# I Absolutely LOVE Indelible Ink! (But It Doesn't Like Me!)

There is one brand
I think is grand
(And this DESPITE the Money)
But I can't <u>drink</u>
Indelible ink!
(It makes MY PEE smell funny!)

Mother Grouse Rhymes
2012 Edition

From: Classic Dazzling Protuberances

## Juliana's Sparkling Wart



The wart on her nose
Is grotesque, heaven knows
(And it would've been counted a blight!)
But her would-be's all notice
(As part of her modus!)
The way that it catches the light!

# TERSE VERSE
# ON VOLCANIC PANIC

Despite the loathsome, acrid fumes
We zoomed and flumed
The gurgling plumes
Till finally
Through the thunderous booms
We raced perspiring
To our rooms
For legumes

# The Girl Could Doze Her Way Through A Jackhammer Concert!



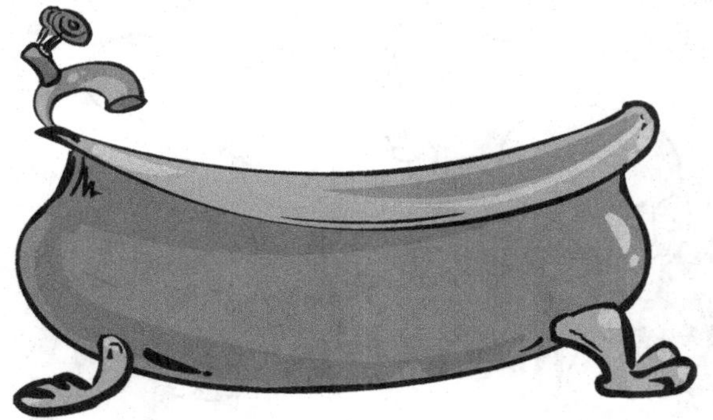

My sister had
A set routine
Whenever she would date
She'd load the sluice
With lilac juice
And then she'd marinate

EDITORIAL

# His Story: A Tragic (Perhaps Careless?) Loss

C: 2011 - Dr. Ron Pataky ---- Custom-Ransom-Notes.com

He lost both his parents
And was so distraught
That he pulled at his scalp
Until hairless!
No WAY could we dun
Had he lost only ONE
But loosing them BOTH
Was just careless!!

# Fifi Olay Attempts Crash; Widow Denies Live Entry

With gin to enhance
Lulu's coffin-side dance
All the guests were served
Cookies and toddy
But when Fifi would crash
Pete's memorial bash
Lulu screamed
**"OVER MY DEAD BODY!"**

# International Prize Awarded Pup For "Fizz" Breakthrough

An inquisitive pup
Had started to think
About bubbles going up in a cup
He noticed that things
Go down in a drink
But the fizzy-stuff always goes up!
An occasional lime
May float for a time
But everything else fails to rise
For his study the pup's
(After downs and some ups)
Been awarded The Noble-Pup Prize!

# Thinking ... As It Relates To the Overly-Strenuous

I occasionally think
About over-work
And the thought of it
Sets me blinkin'

But I seldom give it
Much more thought
For fear
Of over-thinkin'

I've searched all day
It's getting grim
I need a word
For synonym!

# "Hold It, Doc, Do I Have Time For A Quick Smoke?"

Encircling his deathbed
The folks were good-bye-ing
(The <u>mood</u> in the room was quite blue)
He answered the doc's
"Mr. Jones, you are dying"
With: "That is the <u>LAST</u> thing I'd do!"

# I BEG Your Pardon
# May I Extend My Heartfelt!!

I suddenly found
That my tire was bumping
A wobble-prone wheel and all that

I stepped from the car
To see what was thumping
And that's when I noticed your cat

# TWO GUESSES

"It's in one of my hands"
The child confesses
"To make it more harder
I give you two guesses"

# Vodka Roulette Seen As Distinct Relief Possibility

While I'm spilling my guts
She is driving me nuts
Please fetch us two drinks
On the run

Just skip all the noise'n
Make one of 'em poison
And don't even tell me
Which one!

# They're Known Locally As The Skittish Weather Team

Tornados are spotted
We DO have them plotted
It looks like a night
Of pure sorrow

So IF we've returned
We'll convey what we've learned
When the story continues
TOMORROW!!

Have a nice evening...

(WE'RE OUTTA HERE!!)

# Her Bad Habit: Nail-Biting (But NOT On The Fingers!)

Organdy Hales
Always gnawed at her nails
Until friends finally wrapped 'em
In socks

But LATE on her mind
Are the new press-on kind
And she NOW eats 'em straight
From the box!

# Happily For Mrs. Tucker Mr. Nip Was the ONLY One Thusly Beckoned

Nipper and Tucker were battling fools
(At least said the guys who had planned it)
The former came in with inadequate tools
And the boxing-fans barely could stand it!

Tuck pummeled Nip in the very first round
(This Tucker was clearly no faker)
Poor Nip had no zip, plus a slip in his grip
And Nip was recalled by his maker!

# The Bellow Shattered Windows As Far Away As the Parthenon!

Socrates dying
The Senate good-by-ing
T'was surely a <u>MOST</u>
Thankless spot!

When a Senator near
Said "Pssst" in his ear
He LEPT up
And SCREAMED:
I DRANK

# Dyslexia Plagues Group Of Southern Witches!

WHAT THE HECK!! USED SOULS???

Dyslexic witches
Mixed their switches
Meeting in Atlanta

Before the night
Had taken flight
They'd sold their souls
to Santa!!

# Hippocrates, She Groused, Was A Hypocrite!

She would often imply, or outright decry
The greed of the healing profession
The lofty positions of sundry physicians
In time it became an obsession!

She'd sputter and wheeze that all medical fees
Were outrageously high, at best
She neglected to pay her exorcist
Who in turn had her repossessed!

# TEAMWORK



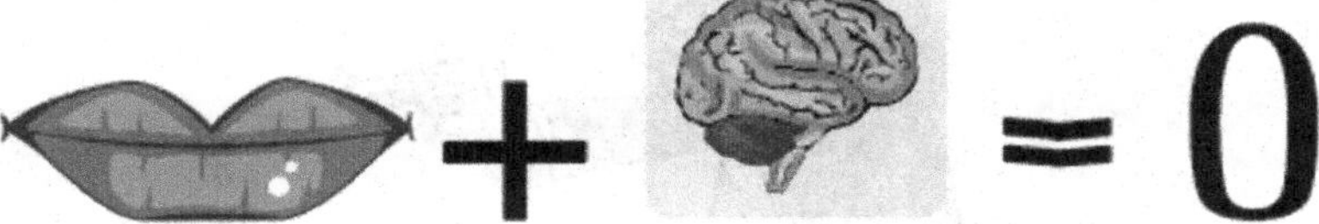


Her hair was like silk
Her complexion like milk
And her smile framed
A delicate gleam-work

But in time it was plain
That her mouth and her brain
Knew naught of the value
Of teamwork!

# MISQUOTED!
# Even The Fine Print!

She said of the kids
"They had pilfered my lids
So I roasted the brats
And I ate 'em!"

But later she'd say
(As they led her away)
"My words were misquoted
Verbatim!"

# Getting the Most Out of Emily Post

C: 2011 - Dr. Ron Pataky --- Custom-Ransom-Notes.com

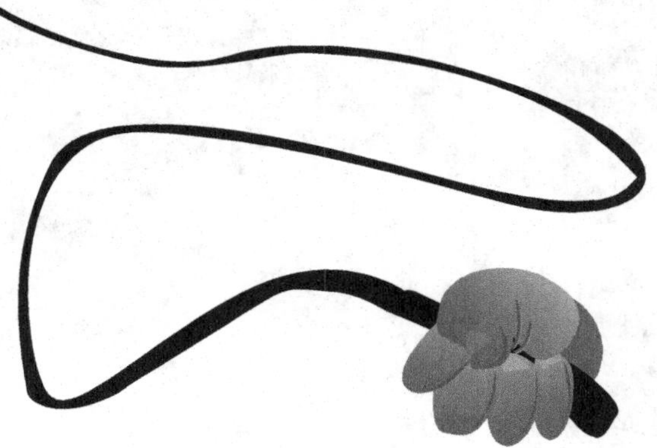

"Fifty-two Lashes!" his honor had gaveled
(The old guy had come close to flipping!)
It was then that the convict HIMSELF came unraveled
Concerning the matter of tipping!

But a kind, caring cellmate
Helped ease the man's dread
(And there's no one who could have been hipper)
On this, protocol is emphatic, he said
One NEVER tips the whipper!

# Mayhem On An Otherwise Midnight Serene

T 'was the night before Christmas
And after his labors
Fred ate a cookie
Then beat up his neighbors
The weatherman did it
No snow to be had
And ... well, I don't know
It just made Fred mad

# Her Mother Taught Her To Order Like A Lady

Brandy's fine...
Perhaps some wine...
Oh my, where should I start?
Some Christmas cheer?
But, please ... no beer!

(Pilsner makes me fart!)

ON KITES: AS THEY MAY PERTAIN
TO THE HEREAFTER

# "High" Has A Unique Usage In Hail-A-Kite Hereafter

Praise be and Hallelujah, Brothers!
Yonder goes Good Sister Blywonker!

Hail-A-Kite rites
In their "Worship of Kites"
Claim death wears a thin,
Kite-like gown

"Our souls catch a breeze
And get stuck in tall trees
And it's hell just to get them
Back down!"

# Mosquitoes, Flies, Wasps... You Name It!

Count 'em, dammit ... TWO!!

Came to "DO IT!"
Noah blew it
THINK about the reach!
E'RE the water
WITH a swatter
AND but two of each!!

# HOSPITAL BLUES

or:

## If it's not too much trouble, Doctor This man over here isn't breathing!

That last buzz made three ... Oh my soul for a pill!
HELEN KELLER could see that I'm desperately ill!
Oh where are the docs when a fellow's in need?
Would a visible pox serve to augment their speed?
Or perhaps if I die (and I will at this pace!)
They will deign with a sigh to reopen my case
At least if I go then, before I awaken
They finally will know then that I wasn't fakin'

# Blue Book On A Used Crook

Scarface Joe
When facing a foe
Would squat on some TNT
So to give him a poke
Would blow a bloke
From here to eternity

Big Al was the same
When annoyances came
He always on dynamite stood!
So go by the book
If you're buying a crook
And always look under the hood!

# Mud Makes Best Bricks And It's CHEAP!

To stop a flood
Use bricks of mud
(Some seeping will not hurt)
It takes no tricks
To make the bricks
And mud is cheap as dirt

# Blue & Fluffy Riddle Baffles Blushing Young Writer

Hint: Classic Abyssinian Blue Fluff

"What's blue and fluffy
Good old Sport?"
The perfect stranger asked
I then assumed
My day was doomed
With such a riddle tasked
I thought of feathers
Even clouds
And lots of puffy stuff
And far from cool
Felt like a fool
When he replied

"BLUE FLUFF"

# When Bird Lovers Ask "Howdaya want that bird?"

C: 2011 – Dr. Ron Pataky --- Custom-Ransom-Notes.com

"A bird in the hand"
Is an adage I've scanned
And when the whole thing
Comes to push

In all future plans
After <u>checking</u> my hands
I'm taking my birds
In a bush!

# IMAGINE!
# All That Activity!
# And Under MY Bed Yet!

From dust do we come
To dust we return
(It's Biblical verse
they are sowing!)
But they better instead
Look under my bed
'Cause SOMEBODY'S
Coming or going!

# Hey ... I Don't NEED No Stinkin' Title!

C: 2011 - Dr. Ron Pataky --- Custom-Ransom-Notes.com

Regarding apathy
I've few thoughts there
I don't know what it means
And I really don't care!

And If You Somehow Miss Me Then

# LEAVE A MESSAGE!!

Bothersome Nick
Always thought he was sick
And was certain that his
Was a hexed life
Said the doctor in warning:
"Take two in the morning
And call me sometime
In the next life"

# She Wasn't Looking For A PERFECT End! Just An END!

Miss Addie bought a clothesline
Her laundry to attend
But when she got the durn thing home
It only had one end!

She stormed back to the merchant
And screamed, "You think you're smart!
You only sold me half a line
Now where's the other part?"

# The Very First Visit To the Daughter at College

C: 2011 - Dr. Ron Pataky ---- Custom-Ransom-Notes.com

What should have been in was out
What should have been out was in
What should have been rolled
In a neatly-packed box
We later found stuffed in a tin

What should have been up was down
What should have been loose would cling
Whom we knew we had taught
"Everything in its place"
Instead said, "I can't find a thing"

What should have been certain was iffy
What should have been serious, funny
The only real word
We consistently heard
Was the unfailing mention of money!

# The Flower-Of-His-Life Was a Lady of Few Word

C: 2011 - Dr. Ron Pataky ---- Custom-Ransom-Notes.com

"I think you're the greatest!
Your sultry eyes glow
For me you're the ONLY one
Kiddo!

"MY life's in the pink!
So what do YOU think?"
And quick as a wink she said
"DITTO!"

# Drifter's Tiff with Sis Is Cause Of Sis' Grimacing Countenance

A drifter named Twist
Was transfixed in the mist
Still miffed at the tiff with his sister
Regardless the gist
Of the riff with his sis
He attempted to kiss her, but missed her
The faces he'd sift
(Giving mostly short shrift)
As he shifted the drift of his pace
Made the sis in the mist
(You recall ... not yet kissed!)
Grimace (while making a face!)

# FEDS ISSUE NEW DIRECTIVE

Director J. Edgar Hooters puts forth edict

Statistics all tell us
That crime is exploding
So pardon if I have my say
Perhaps it is time
That we federalize crime
Cause then sure as hell
It won't pay!

J. Edgar Hooters, Director
Federal Bureau of Investilaguibba

# There's Tom! Right There! Eight Seventy First From The Left In The 14-Thousandth Row!



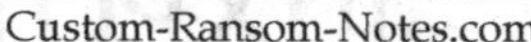

The billions of felines

Extant in the world
Are causing our lenses constricture
We're trying to wangle

A super wide-angle
And hoping to get a group picture!

# JUXPOTASITION:
## As It Relates to Lysdexia



## Assorted Mixaphors

An apple a day
Brings flowers in May
And a stitch that is late
Is regretted
Wisdom is time
Though I think in this rhyme
My mixaphors somehow
Got metted!

# YEA AND NAY TIPS FOR FAST ONE-WAY TRIPS

Condensed from

AMAZONIA: A QUICK WRAP

By the late Hyman "Hy" Strung

Abstain from fresh fruits
(You CAN eat boiled roots)

Lakes aren't for swimmin'
Do NOT touch the women

When in the interior
You WILL be inferior

The water's just fair
Do NOT breathe the air

Don't bother to pack
(You AIN'T comin' back!)

# You CAN Assess a Dame By Her Keyboard Inclinating!



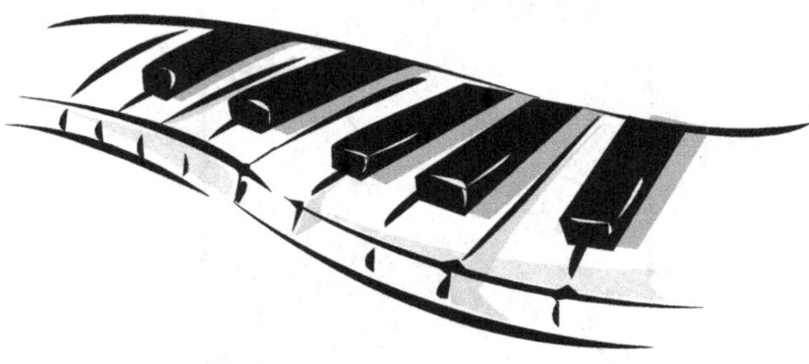

I try to rate
The dames I date
And find (despite nay-sayers)
That some are upright
Some are grand
And SOME
Are merely players!

# On My Euphoric Discovery That I'm a Boy-Child



By Jamie C.
Class 2 - Miss Moofy

My big brother Tommy has one, too!

Imagine my exuberance
On spotting a protuberance!

# Additionally - Burial Plots
# Why Own When You Can Rent?

Consider, for example, amortization:
How long do you and the missus plan on being dead?

## As it comes to the end
## Please consider our credo:

## BURY YOUR FRIEND
## IN A RENTED TUXEDO!

ADVERTISEMENT

Brought to you
by
Eternity Renters & Sons
[or Survivors]

ATT: SOGGY WHISTLE AFICIONADOS!

# Know A Soggy Whistle When You See It??



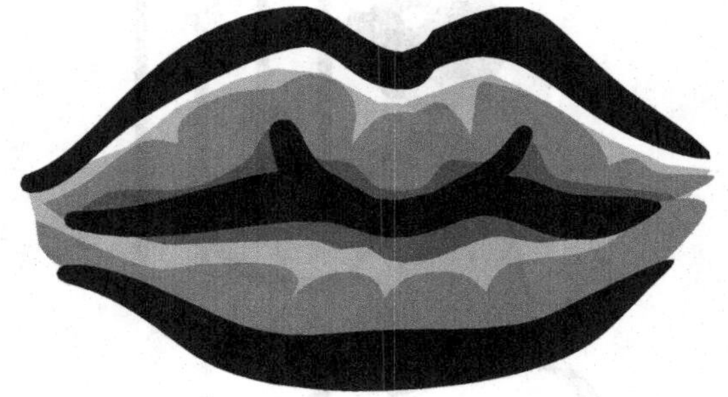

One VERY soggy whistle!

Hildagarde Schlissel
When wetting her whistle
(Will pucker until she gets groggy)
Then she'll say (without bliss)
When asked for a kiss
"I CAN'T NOW ...
MY WHISTLE IS SOGGY!!"

# IS STERILIZATION THE ANSWER FOR THE CONDEMNED?

Death row reps
Have taken steps
Predicting those who plead'll
Ask they heed
Who DO the deed
First, sterilize the needle!

# Had I NOT Done It
# It Would Have Been Late Anyway!

(Photosynthesis helped somewhat, but on a VERY limited basis)

I thought that if I did it
And providing no one hid it
The only question then
Would be just when
But when I finally did it
(Ostensibly to rid it!)
Was when I knew
I should have done it then!

# ARCHEOLOGY

An incredible fact
Has just been uncovered
In documents recently found
An ounce of prevention
We've just discovered
Was one-sixteenth of a pound!

# NAMETITE

## Protecting Your Precious Name Is Our TERMINAL Priority!!

We seal it in tents
Then surround it with fence
Then we see that steel walls are erected
We dig a deep moat
On the surface to float
All the poisonous snakes we've collected
For the very last touch
There are bear-traps and such
(Plus the ten million volts we've connected)
When finished we claim
That for certain your NAME
For the next SEVERAL months is protected!

# A SENTIMENTAL LOSS IS THE ABSOLUTE WORST!

A pickpocket deft
With a very light touch
Has near brought my family to tears!

It's not the we miss
The wallet so much
But the money's been with us for years!

# And THEN ...
# The Meatball Came Along!

You're gonna make WHAT???

The year that sausage
Was invented
Porcine carnage
Consequented

# and now ... respectfully a question for the pope

C: 2011 - Dr. Ron Pataky ---- Custom-Ransom-Notes.com

The Gregorian calendar, named for Pope Greg
Gave us a guide neither puzzling nor vague
And yet there are persons for whom in their musing
Are questions aplenty attached to its using

What kind of mind after all could conceive
A screwed-up concoction that clearly would leave
A shortage of dates set aside for our fun days
Yet fully a **SEVENTH** of each life to Mondays??

# Slicing Through The Near-Mythical Murk Of History

Listen my children
and you shall hear
the ugly tale
of Paul Revere

He boozed despite warning
Till swacked as could be
And that's why the British
Now own Tennessee!

# Some Perplexing Pickle THIS Particular Peter's In!



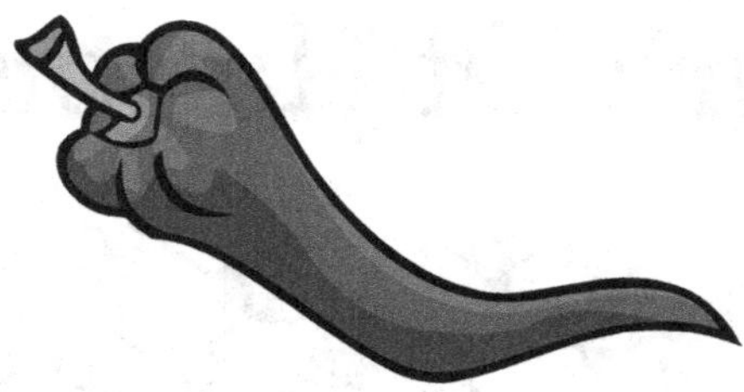

Peter Piper, they say
Picked pickled peppers
But somewhere
Someone's been tricked

For there's simply no pepper
Extant in the world
That is pickled
Before it is picked

'Course it could be the rhyme
Was composed at a time
When the poet
Was just feeling tickled

Or it could be, too
(If the story is true)
That the poet himself
Was pickled!

# Vengeance Is Mine Sayeth the Poodle

Gretel would yodel
To rattle her poodle
(Two notes and the puppy would scat!)
While Gretel ate strudel
It entered pup's noodle
To daintily poop in her hat

## He More-Or-Less Poo-Pooed Her "Prehistoric Dirt" As Well!

Hell's bells, ol' Ferdy Dinglewomp uses 'em every day!

She traveled the fairs
Selling petrified squares
(When it came to the con she was slick!)

Said a lad, from the blue
"Don't known about you
But back home we know it as brick!"

# WHAT I THINK SHE'S SAYING IS THAT A COOL SNORT TASTES DANDY ON A HOT DAY

Priscilla Potter-Bipple
Claims a now-and-then small sip'll
"Cool your jibbles
When your siblings like it hot"
"As a willow's mighty supple
So to cool and tip one up'll
Make it seem a bit of heaven
When it's not!"

<u>CLASSIFIEDS</u>

# Did Anyone SEE Our Notes?

At a recent Boy Scout Jamboree
Some somebody lost the notes
And as a result
There's no one knows
The results of the various votes

So as to the outcome there isn't a hint
Concerning the question of whether
Our fires should be made
By the banging of flint
Or by rubbing two Boy Scouts together

# A Quick Electrical Seminar Might've Helped Plenty!

To his buddy the convict
Enroute to the chair
"May you have the reward
That is due you
"Do not feel defeated
Indeed when you're seated
BE CHEERFUL!
AND MORE POWER TO YOU!"

# Not Even Tragedy Tempts Faith of Mom

Even though
The grief might flow
His mother was devout
"You'd better pray"
He'd hear her say
"That awful SPOT comes out!"

# MATRIMONIAL LISTINGS

Constance Nipper, Proprietor

# WEEKLY SPECIAL

She's a steal
Terrific deal
Tiny, mousy clerk
Price is cut
Great bargain but
She's going to need some work

# ON THE PANGINGS OF SOLITUDE

Aloneliness

There stood I
An only child
As lonely as lonely could be
I only had two
Make-believe friends
And they wouldn't play with me!

# LIBRARY DIRECTIONS

You've PASSED "Conjunctions"
Right next to "Compunctions"
There under the red "Exit" light!
What you want is "Functions"
Near "Funk," before "Unctions"
'Bout twenty feet down on your right!

# Give the Old Gal Credit
# She Just Keeps Hangin' In There!

Mona Lisa lives in the Louvre
She pays no rent
Nor will she move
Just hangs around there all the while
Wearing that silly pedestrian smile

But don't be quick
In judging this dame
What she lacks in talent's
Made up by fame
Indeed to possess this fading flower
Would cost you <u>more</u>
Than the Eiffel Tower!

# THUMPINGLY, RESOUNDINGLY & EMPHATICALLY NOCTURNAL

Gendarmes merely followed the bouncing balls

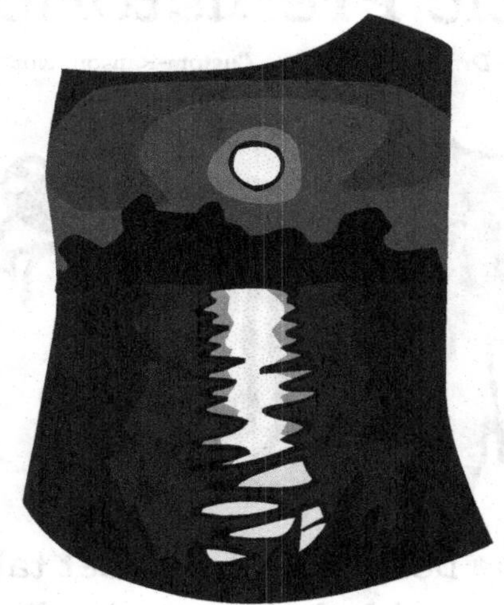



Quaint Lucretia Whifflestump
Had several balls with which to bump
As nightly she'd cavort
Out on the terrace

The balls would echo off the stones
'Gainst urgent rings of many phones
Awakening the sleep streets
Of Paris!

# Archeological Dig Reveals Gigantic Prehistoric Bear

The beast stood ten feet tall
Roughly half a ton in all
And ERECT he was
[Attentive as a Mantis!]

The researchers stacked the bones
With an eye towards future clones
And they <u>named</u> the creature
Ursi Pissi-pantus!

# About That Time, MOST Guys Would've Evaporated Like Mornin' Burn-Off!!

Original David Slingshot
Can Be Seen at the
Goliath Museum – New Philisteenia

David could dig
This Goliath was BIG!
[And DAVID would be all alone!]
The final off-kissing:
"Our Howitzer's missing...
You'll have to make do
With a stone!!"

(OH, MY!)

# Village Creep Protected ONLY By Threat of Epidingis Infestation

Fustus "Bumps" Renn
Was a toad among men
A creature with heart
Kin to quartz

Though most
Would have bashed him
And throttled and thrashed him
They knew that to TOUCH him
Meant warts!

# TOURIST WARNING!

## SPEED LIMIT - 3 MPH



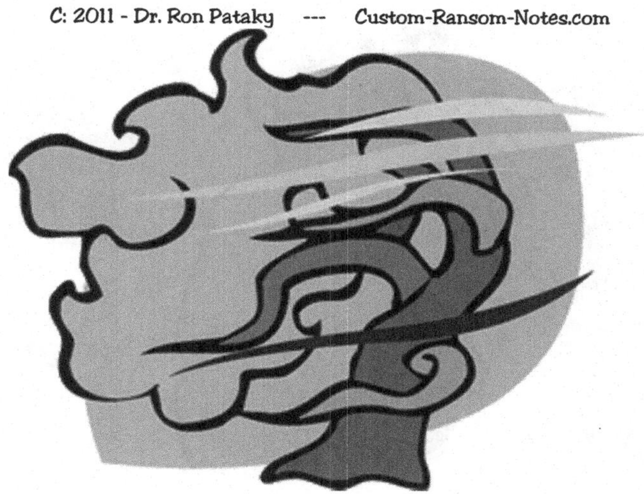

Top Of sky
Can tumble some
Filling town with fuzz
Doesn't happen
All the time
But tricky when it does!

# THEY SAY! And They SAY They Will Say Again!!

They say he's inspired, they say Denmark's wild
They say she was fired because she's with child
They say back-bay oysters libidos enhance
They say Ahmed cloisters his harem in France
They say India's swell IF you bypass Bombay
By the way who the

**HELL**

Are these nebulous they?

# Where IS The Fuzz? And WILL The Fuzz Be As It Was?

A dashing bear was Fuzzy Wuz
But Fuzzy Wuz, he had no fuzz
Rather, though, than rave and rant
He went and had a fuzz implant

Alas, he failed to pay the fee
Despite fine fuzz (which all could see)
And as the docs feel they've been burned
They want the now-used fuzz returned

# With Such Simple Directions WHY Don't They Ever Show Up?

Three miles (or more)
Past the beer and bait store
You turn when you pass a red car

When you see a small Basset
Slow down lest you pass it
Which means that you've traveled too far

There's a cat on the right
(On the left if it's night)
By a church (and you could see a mourner)

The next road is ours
With some nondescript flowers
(And MAYBE a deer on the corner!)

# AUTOBIOGRAPHY



Feebis W. Bunkinlode

AUTHENTIC DEATH MASK - 2001

I've thought a bunch since missing lunch
About my lengthy life
I had some chairs, a couch somewheres
(And think I had a wife)

There was this job (a nasty mob)
And pay I think I got
Some cars on roads, and laundry loads
And dust (I think a lot!)

Through hazy lids, I see some kids
And two look much like me
I think I have some names on file
If only I could see

There was a yard, a driveway tarred
And scenes of puppy-petting
I hate to cut, would say more but
I'm fearful of forgetting

# Home Grown Fella ...
# Solid Roots & Everything!

When she was young
And brimming with hope
She developed a marvelous plan
She made the decision
To grow her own dope!
So she went out and planted
A man!

# Hell, I Can't Help It If I'm Appearancely-Challenged!

I have to say
(With minimal scorn)
I have a handsome brother!

Came the day
That I was born
The doctor slapped my mother!

<u>STUPID MEN TRICKS</u>

# Deputies Let 'Em Sleep It Off In Local Pig Shacks!

Hey! Thanks for bringin' the booze, Fellas!

Four local goons
Spend their nights in saloons
(Though they promise their wives
That they won't)

So how, full of foam
Do they ever get home??
The sheriff says simply,
"They don't!"

# And, You're Not Actually Reading This!

C: 2011 - Dr. Ron Pataky --- Custom-Ransom-Notes.com

Life is a myth
All "without" is "with"
And the sky's losing ground
To the sea
It's NOT today's date
And three and two's eight

(And nobody knows it but me!)

# VANITY'S FARE

She was, as a child
Both gorgeous and cunning
So modesty hadn't a chance

Her image in windows
She found to be stunning
Thus kindling a lifelong romance

She crinkled at last
(All that "fun" in the sun!)
And she's no longer chased by the men

And her rusty old parts?
Well, they now barely run
As her "now" pays the price of her "then"

# AFTER DIVORCE

C: 2011 - Dr. Ron Pataky --- Custom-Ransom-Notes.com

## A Plan for Life

When I'm single at last
I will have me a blast
And I'll play like my best friend is Cupid!

I will get my own dump
Spend more time with the plump
And I'll LEARN, picking brains of the stupid!

I will chuck all my fears
In my middle-aged years
And I'll write an occasional rhyme

And then (despite mold)
I'll smell <u>nice</u> when I'm old!
And I <u>will</u> be deceased when it's time!

# His Spinster-Friend Didn't Mind The Tic... But She Had A Problem With Him Being So Vertically-Challenged

Old-Timer Nick
Had a visible tic
But he tried every trick
just to court her
He'd spin round and round
Until screwed in the ground
But the exercise
just made him shorter

# All Members of Congress Should Be Limited To TWO Terms!

TWO terms should be
The limit in Congress
A plan guaranteed
Not to fail
The first one should be
The TIME spent in Congress
The second
A few years in jail!

# Oh, And I May Have To Be Out The Entire Week



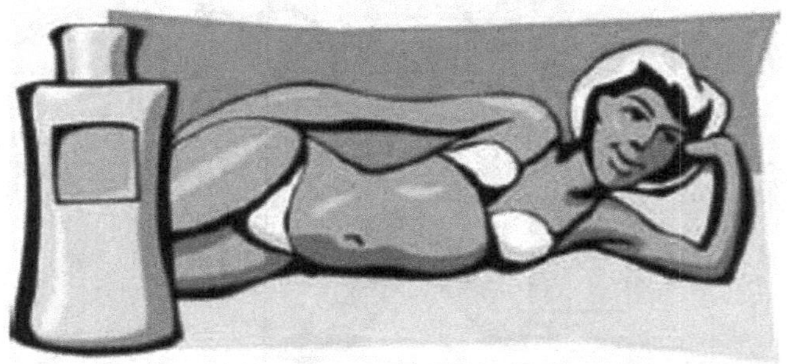

She'd used up all her sick leave
Missing one more caused her dread
But with the dawn
A bulb came on
"I think I'll call in dead!"

# Artist Solemnly Declares

# VERTIGO

## Its Own Reward!

Among her roles
She claims her goal's
"To chaos to surrender"
She calls her hope
**"KALEIDOSCOPE"**
or
**"FEATHERS IN A BLENDER"**

## Proof (Finally!) That Most ALL Heels Lack Souls!

Walk a full mile
In the other guys shoes
If judgment is going to be fair!

THEN when you judge
You're a mile away
And MAYBE can sell your old pair!

# Hey, Kid ... Someday YOU Might Want To Be NINETY!!

WHOA!

"Who would WANT
To be eighty-five?"
(The teenager seemed
to deplore)
To me (off the cuff)
It seemed clear enough:
"Someone who's
eighty-four!!"

# On the Equitable Distribution Of Left-Over Leftovers

Good things may come
To those who wait
Conserving their mind
And their muscle
But only the things
That are left by the gate
By the sick, greedy bastards
Who hustle!

<u>OBITUARY</u>

# Remembering Sir Cyril Sumppump

 Custom-Ransom-Notes.com

1921-2009

He invented the belch
Mac 'n Cheese and the "vowel"
Inflated dart boards
And the water-proof towel

# Check It Out, Buzwald
# Four Corners minus ONE = 3

There are 4 corners marked in a square
Which leads neither here nor to there
But take away one
And your square is undone
Which triangles call only fair

# We All Know That Toddlers Require Lots of Help

For toddlers who cling
Support is the thing
And it's true both for boys
And the ladies
It happens for fun
When we're about one
And then once again
In our eighties

# A Few Wait ... !
# And Wonder About Rule 2

There are two basic rules
Which in life must be met
(At least so the best minds
Have reckoned)

The FIRST is to grab
Everything you can get

(And nobody knows the second!)

# Tuesday-Type Hot New Item On World Convention Market!

The NEWEST convention
Will center on Tuesday
Engendering groans
To the rafter

EACH Tuesday, they say
Will be honored that way
AS WILL EVERY
DAMNED TUESDAY
THERE-AFTER!

A station in Texas
Has got it together
They've labeled
Their forecasting

**"ACCU-HUNCH WEATHER"**

# Barking Around the Clock Earns Muffy No Kudos At All!

Muffy, though freezing
(Whose hobby was sneezing)
Decided to fold in some coughing

She went to the doctor
Who suddenly socked her
With news there was strep in the offing

He took a deep listen
Found several thumps missin'
Then said that her cough wasn't right

As she glared at the doc
She said, "What a crock...
"And after I practiced all night?"

# A MESSAGE FOR SPRING

For thousands of years
Spanning laughter and tears
We have raved of our youth and its brawn
But the horrible truth
Is that most of our youth
Has aged, and has died, and is gone!

Have a wonderful day!

# Ya Only Got ONE Back!
# Hernias Are a Dime a Dozen!

And she's a pretty hefty load, too!

You will see when you sway
As you lift the wrong way
A lesson that quickly
Will learn ya

To plan an attack
That does NOT use your back
You balance the load
On your hernia!

# They Say The Dude Was Trapped For Two FULL Days!

Citizens snickered
At Bert -- who was snockered!
(He'd no notion
Where the wall'd been!)
But he POKED (on a roll!)
'Round a telephone pole
And concluded
That he was walled-IN !

# Coincidentally, They Missed The Exact SAME Questions!

Teddy had flunked
And WHY was it so?
It seems he was caught in a lie
The boy to his right
Wrote, "I do not know""
And Teddy wrote, "Neither do I""

# Slobberers into Veritable Soot Is Verdict of Peruvian Court

People who slobber
Are being unraveled
According to news from Peru
"It's high time to clobber
A jurist had gaveled
The drool-shoddy ways of a few!
"And after they've laid
In a sweet marinade
We'll swing 'em from pulleys on high
"And we'll then cut them down
In the center of town
And we'll burn 'em to soot
When they're dry!"

ON LEARNING FROM THE BIRDS

# Thrushes, Warblers, Titmice Swallows ... You Name 'Em

Who me? I'm doin' life

Old birds
Teach their young birds
(And they perch on every word!)
Window glass
You bet your ass
Is better seen than heard!

# CATASTROPHIC NEWS TODAY!

Hurricane Zsa Zsa
Makes landfall tonight
Folks'll clamor for shelter in vain
The Bureau predicts
One hell of a fright!
But we WILL get
Some much-needed rain!!

And now this word from Guppo's Cistern's

# VERDICT: THE LION PIT AT PRECISELY IX A.M!

Consider the plight
Of the misinformed slave
Whose ignorance sealed his fate
Who scrawled on the walls
Of cave after cave
That XI less VI equals VIII!

# There's Just NO Excuse At All For This INCESSANT Dithering!

C: 2011 – Dr. Ron Pataky ---- Custom-Ransom-Notes.com

As our winter clouds cling
Does this late frost in spring
Find the morning
With small flowers withered

We have warned them before
On this very same score
It's what HAPPENS
When heaven has dithered!!

# Such EXCESSIVE Silence COULD'VE brought the Cops!

The silence was loud
We were very near cowed
(Though a few claimed
It just didn't matter)
But WE were not proud
Of a silence THAT loud
So we drowned it
In meaningless chatter!

# SALOME LOSES PICK AFTER REALLY LAME DANCE

"She can make ANY choice"
(T'was the King's mighty voice)
But the dance that she did
Was a bum one
"Oh my goodness," she cried
(With her first choice denied)
"Then, bring me the head, please
Of **SOMEONE**!!

# There's Just No Way You'd <u>EVER</u> Hear The Phrase "Drape The Dude Till It Really, Really HURTS!!"

<u>VOTE</u>

FOR SHERIFF "KNICKERS" GILDENBONGLE

"Hanged until **<u>DEAD</u>**!"
Is what the judge said
But the folks in the town
Wanted more!

"**<u>MORE</u>**?!!" screamed the crook
"It is **<u>NOT</u>** in the book
To be 'Hanged by the neck
Until **<u>SORE</u>** !!' "

# Mottos May Come and Go; But So Do Trolleys and Zits

"Help the Inept"
Is a motto I've kept
And I'm pleased as pure punch
At its keptness

Though I've failed and been burned
Through my failing I've learned
Just how swept up I am
With ineptness!

# Their AAA Guide Had <u>Told</u> Them The Front Desk Closes Nightly At Ten!

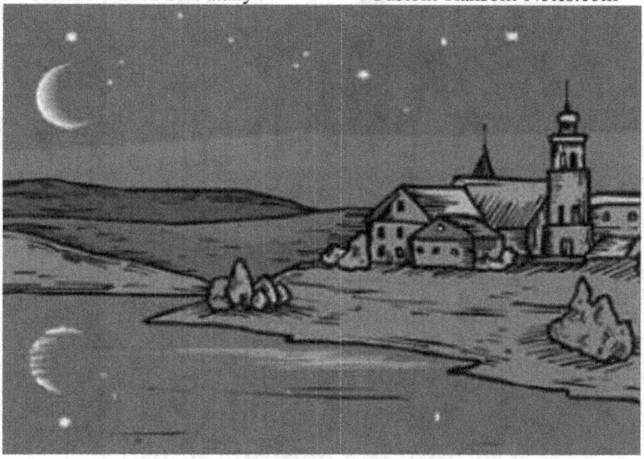

They were amazed to learn
that <u>the</u> <u>whole</u> <u>place</u> shuts down about then!

Nearing death did she smile
At the truth she's been told
That Heaven would be
<u>SUCH</u> a sight!

But it really got old
Sleeping out in the cold
When they flew in there
TOO LATE AT NIGHT!

# <u>Nasturtium Pills Guaranteed To Ease Campus Loads</u>

**Maximum Occupancy: 9**

Havinghill's
Nasturtium Pills
Are now the campus hottie
They loosen bowels
Amidst the howls
As students hit the potty
Their "Potty Time"
Involves a climb
To get atop the toilet
And then a glut
Of
POTTY BUTT
With warning then to boil it!

# Look Out, Delbert!

# It's Comin' BACK!!



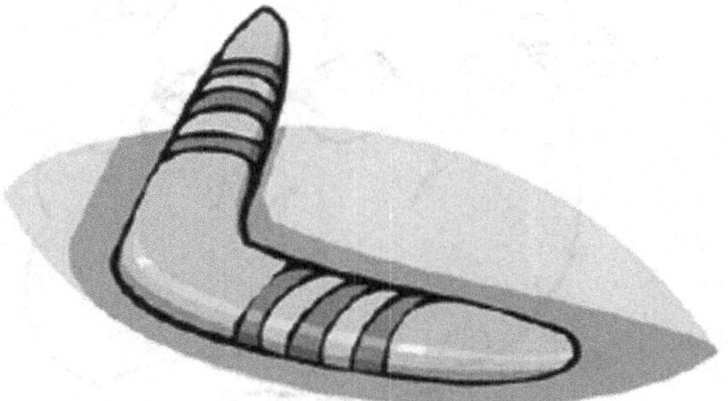

That things can come back to haunt us
Is a truth that is almost anointed
That why it's not wise
To tell people lies
And it's why boomerangs
Aren't pointed

# Heifer's Disappearance Now Blamed on Mystery Bull

What do we do now
As concerns the missing cow
(The bull had pulled all strings
That he could pull!)
With his bull-emotions full
He performed another pull
Then he softly sobbed
"She's met another bull"

# Imagine the Time-Saving When Seeking Directions From a Stranger!

**DUH!**

I think stupid people
Should have to wear signs
(Though it might be a turn-off
For Cupid)

That way, on approach
You can say, reading lines
"Oh, pardon,
I see that you're stupid"

# SHE SAYS WE MAY EVEN GET A NEW PORCH SCREEN!

When moppin' the kitchen
I oft think of switchin'
The various roles with my spouse

Right now I decide
If we go for a ride
And SHE if we buy a new house!

The way that it stands
Is that I suggest plans
On where we <u>might</u> groove with HER car

I wash the clothes
But only SHE knows
If we're planning to MOVE (and how far!)

# Oooo-kay ... Take THAT You Wicked, Wicked Woman!

**When her obstinate stance**
**Took my rage**
**To new heights**
**I growled at her plants**
**And mixed colors**
**With whites!**

# Multiple Listing By Multiple Personalities

We think that we shall never see
A cuter six
Than you and me
When we're alone, what do we do?
We list for you
And you
And you
When we're away, we hope you'll be
Listing for Me
And Me

**[And don't forget me!!]**

# A Palpitating First for Both Mother AND Child!!

Jill saw
On the board
The umbilical cord
And she stared at her mom
On the table
Then she whispered in awe
Of the wonder she saw:

**"DO NEW BABIES COME
WITH CABLE??"**

# Wow! Meat for All 23 of Us And Scrumptious Gravy For a Month or More!

Great Gravy! Even Finney's
Uncle Sagamore chipped in!

Let's roast the Fat Guy, said Buck to the boys
And quickly a bunch of us chased him
To get Fat Guy pinned, we ran like the wind
Till most of us thought we could taste him

We cornered Fat Guy (who muttered "Oh my!")
And some felt a tinge when we faced him
But despite a few sighs, it did take six guys
Merely to rotate and baste him!

ON THE PRACTICAL ENTERTAINING
OF UNEXPECTED SIMIANS

# The Knicks Are Out of Town And the Library Closes Early

And you can't get in Sardi's at all without pants!

I found this darling monkey
And so took him to the zoo
When evening came I felt a bit
Of groovy

Tomorrow is another day
And scheduling is due
I'm thinking I may take him
To a movie!

# Broth Virtually Certain When Conditions Are Met

When veggies are cleaned
From the garden just gleaned
And tumbled with meat from a cloth

And seasoned for fun
And then boiled until done
It is difficult not to make broth

# <u>Catered Funerals New Rage Amongst Hip Boomer Crowd</u>

**(See our ad in this month's Sassy-Plung)**

We're catering bereavement
For those tender funeral times
A dirge for you, and flowers too
And tender, caring rhymes

A handsome hearse
Some soothing verse
(Our pastors are terrif!)

And if it leads
To special needs
We <u>can</u> provide a stiff!

**And if you lack**
**Financial grace**
**We gladly <u>rent</u>**
**Eternal Space!**

# Al, Of Course, Claimed <u>HE</u> Was With the Horse!

A hung-over dope
And a scoot-about mope
Skedaddled into the corral
The sheriff, of course
Tried to vacate the horse
Who quickly advised
"I'm with Al!"

**EXPRESS NEWS FROM THE ORIENT**

# Great Wall of China Moved To New Location!

**Making space for a mall**
**We have moved the Great Wall**
**And Wal-Mart is filled with elation**

**Suspended by wire**
**It's now two feet higher**
**Than t'were at it's former location**

**But problems arose**
**(And they will, heaven knows!)**
**When the one faction thought it too seedy**

**With the merchants and all**
**And with billboards so tall**
**And KA-PLASTERED with Chinese graffiti!**

# And I Confess:
# I AM a Little Unsteady!

I trust you can see
You must NOT mess with me!
I can be quite nasty, to wit:
Though quite soon I will
Have a license to kill
I DO have a learner's permit

# Not Only Meat, But Gravy For a Month or More!



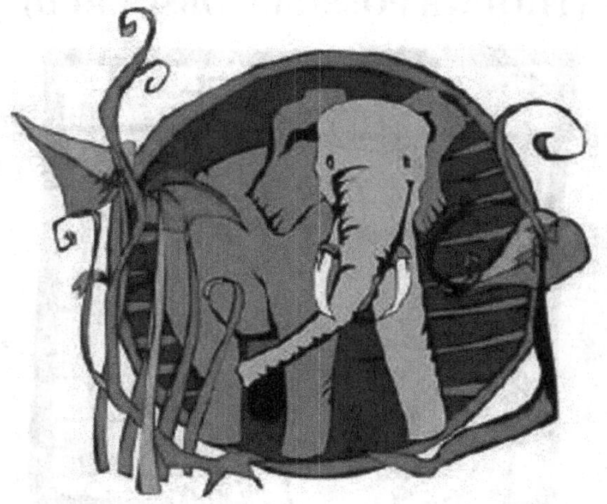

* Just one SINGLE elephant!

The cannibals were starving
The summer had been hard
Nor was there in the land
A living creature! *

A voice said "All is fine
We're the Gods and we're divine
And we're giving you this day
A chubby preacher!"

# MOST CLOUDS DO HAVE A SILVER LINING

## (THOUGH POSSIBLY OBSCURED)

He was sentenced through tears
To a "hard" ninety years
But he managed to smile
through the strife

He said, "It's a curse
But it might have been worse
He could easily
have given me life!"

## His Curmudgeon Pappy Made It Even Worse: 'Get Ahead, Son - Every BODY Needs One!' (Yuk Chortle Yuk Yuk)

Guinness would be knighted
He had the title sighted
And he planned to keep his clippings by his bed

But when the Queen upended
And her slippery sword descended
It separated Guinness from his head

So when he hit the gravel
(On deciding he would travel)
He quickly had some trouble at the border

His body weight was off a bit
But then the thing that REALLY hit
Was Guinness was eleven inches shorter!

***"She knew too much," claims rowdy***

# Cops Tase $7^{th}$ Grader; Rascal Dragged Away In Chains

A boy slew his seventh grade teacher
And responding to motives and such
Said, "I hardly rejoice
But I had no real choice
The lady just knew too much!"

# Alas, However, Young Village Men Kept Disappearing At A Truly Alarming Rate

**Some guys couldn't believe their eyes!**

Thumbelina Whistlestick
Would every month a suitor pick
To nail above the headboard in her bedroom

In time the space would not suffice
For keeping spacing spacely nice
For lack of what appeared to be the head-room

She had her ceiling put on poles
Thus tripling ceiling spatial roles
While guaranteeing they would pass inspection

And upped her picks to once a week (!)
Whilst soon the slightest casual peek
Would demonstrate a rather nice collection!

# Steam Pump Thrombs At Steadified 72 BPMs

C: 2011 – Dr. Ron Pataky ---- Custom-Ransom-Notes.com

Clyde, you can bet'll
Stay close to the kettle
While noting a pulse
"On the beam"

The small metal kettle
Keeps Clyde in fine fettle
(His pacemaker's powered
By steam!)

# Spent Batteries Strewn Everywhere? Here's a Thought!



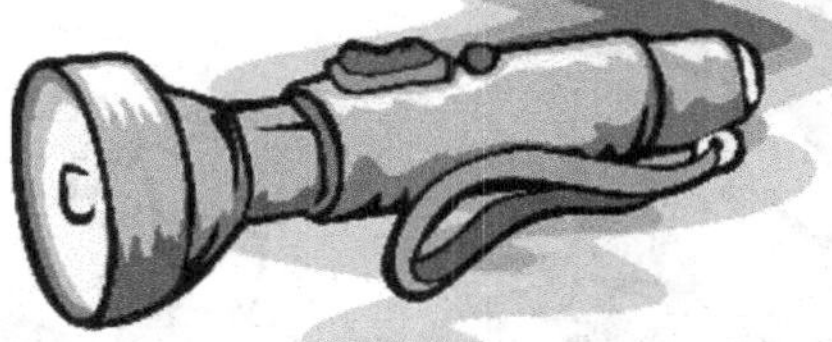

A flashlight
Is the cure for dark
And also, it is said

A super place
For storing them
When batteries are dead!

# I No Longer Find That Tranquility Necessarily Sucks

Don't know about you
But I've given up fighting
And now, though it's new
I find boredom exciting

# Loose Translation From "Yangtze Herbal Curses"

Not care for your boss?
Put curse on his calm
Sneak hot pepper sauce
In posterior balm

# Thought for the Day

"Let's Brighten Our World!"

Should you meet a fellow man
Wearing a frown
Light one single candle
And burn his ass down!

# Ollie Oglethorpe Simply Devoured The Fricaseed Ear Nubbins!

Lettie Ledbetter was nobody's fool
The night that she carved up the fowl
The slow-basted carcass
Made all the fools drool
(But the bird on the plate was an OWL!!)

She carved and she slivered
Then passed it with glee
As aromas fair tickled each nose
Not a peep did she speak
Of the bird's pedigree
As SHE daintily nibbled the toes

# Talk About a Square Cork In A Triangular Fissure!

A parallel universe
Caught my attention
And thusly my lobals
Were sparked

And though somewhat square
I am now living there
(Although I am
Diagonally parked!)

**YOUR FLORAL NEWS**

# Elderly Wrinkled Woman Soars Proudly Across Convention Stage

Ignoring reporters completely
the following Sunday

Great-Granny Fay
Streaked a flower display
And most there assumed
A mirage
Till she won (in her size)
The First SENIOR Prize
For the cleverest
Old Dried Corsage

# Come Nightfall She Now Must Go Next Door For Beddy-Bye!

Jewel would drool
When in her pool
Without her nasal winches

And hot or not
When she forgot
The pool would rise six inches!

The day would come
(With help of Rum!)
And tons of surface head room

When she'd confess
That drool excess
Had re-aligned her bedroom

# Meet Cyrus: A Dude With A Distinct Sink-Wish

A pessimist gent
Was encased in cement
While friends took him out in the boat
"You've got your wish, Cy
You finally will die"
"YEH RIGHT!
And what if I FLOAT?"

**HEALTH UPDATE**

# Hardening Of the Farteries



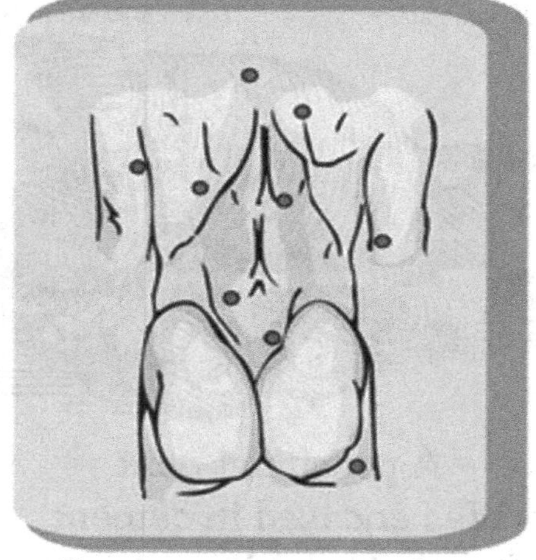

Fartery pressure points
for expelling steel-like clumplings

Hardening
Of the Farteries
Has folks down in the dumps
Symptoms feel
Like tongs of steel
Clamped way up in their rumps

# Partial-Day Wage Fans Fury Of Doomed Roman Slave

Linnaeus rumored thoroughly pissed at prospect

Yazza, guys, breakfast at 10!

~ ~ ~ ~ ~ ~ ~

He was being paid per diem
In the Roman Coliseum
And he kept a running tally
'Midst his pages
But the lions in the pen
Would be FED the dude at ten!
Which would mean that day
He'd get but partial wages!

# The Ever-Looming Curse of Ain't-ness



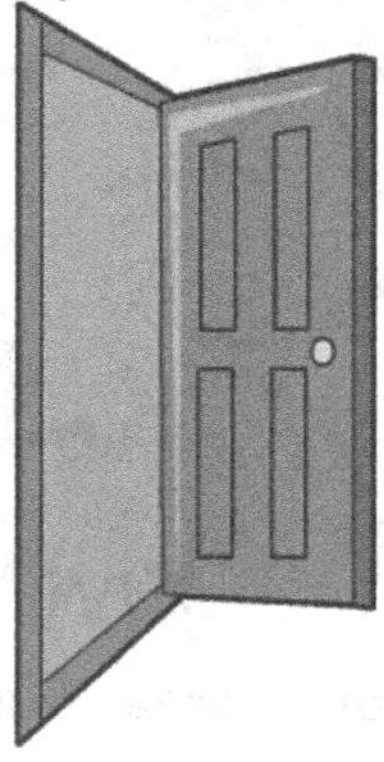

There surely should be more to life
A way to up the score
A door through which
Good conquers strife
And through which there is more

A door with promise full of hope
A door both calm and quaint
A door whose frame
My heart might grope
But what the hell … there ain't!

**New from Mercer Products**

# Powdered Air!

***Coming to supermarkets everywhere June 1***



## ALSO NEW!

Pesky gust?
Try pickled dust
Just place upon the sill
Its pungence flows
Throughout your nose
With slightest hint of dill!*

*Dill Extra

# It's One Gallery EVERYONE Should Have On Hand!

Everyone
Should keep on hand
Their photos for the foyer
The ten most wanted
In the land
AND EVERY ONE
A LAWYER!

# In a Dire, Lifelong Search For An Acceptable Palate

When e're it slipped
My lips, they dripped
And lo, I heard a twang

My voice went up
About a cup
And thus, with this, I sang

A chunky mass
(This, too, would pass)
Proscruded with a bang

As vocals peaked
T'was then I creaked
O, What a Webbled Tang!

# After All This Time Maybe It DOES Freeze In July?

**Not to fret, they say,**
**Poppinlocher has been summoned from the Alps!**

The atomic clock
Keeps time for the world
A permanent, global delight
But how do we know
(Maybe fast, maybe slow?)
That the <u>ONLY</u>
such timepiece
**IS RIGHT??**

# There's a Little Bit Of Ourselves In Each of Us!

I scarcely need to mention
That it's come to my attention
That the deeper of "retention"
Means "to keep"

I think about it all the day
In every angled, shaded way
And often mull it over
In my sleep!

I've mangled 'bout a million books
Midst dropsied and suspicious looks
From dippy folks who simply
Do not get it

And print a tract 'about every hour
(Purpose being to give me power)
On paper that is dull
Until I wet it!

And finally
While I still can budge
I close my eyes
And pray for fudge!

# A VERY SERIOUS POME

By Ronald Pataky

Once in our town
Lived a Cyclops Boy
Whose eyesight
was not what it should be

So his dear daddy bought him
An eyeglass to wear
To show him what good eyesight
could be!

But the boys in our town
Could be very cruel
Especially two bullies
with blue eyes

Who beat him in games
And called him weird names
The most hurtful of which was
"TWO EYES"

# NOTHING's Quite As Bad As Tired, Aching Latex!

Rubber Ducky in a tub
Rubber Ducky needs a rub
Ducky needs the rubbie for
Ducky's rubber's AWFUL sore!

# What Say We Get Together Later For Some Strained Beets?

Regarding foul tempers
I've little to say
So button your yap
And get out'a my way!

This is written in code.

See if you can unlock Ezzy's secret

(HINT: The clues are in a different poem!!)

Esmerelda Fraim
Was a USER-FRIENDLY dame
Who specialized in lying to her parents!

The day she snuck around the barn
And slipped a bit and whispered, "Darn"
T'was spotted by her little brother Clarence

Poopy Clarence did his thing
And gave their Pa a hasty ring
And tattled to the tune of "Drop a Bomb"

And angry Papa raced outside
With trusty belt for Ezzy's hide
Which left her bruised and limping for the prom

# He <u>ALSO</u> Bought
# A Huge Pile of Corroded Shingles
# Titled
# "DANGER ... KEEP OFF!"

A gallery guard
Parked the truck in the yard
And carried a frame through the door

Two guys (thanks to peeling)
Were painting the ceiling
And splattered some paint on the floor

As the empty frame stayed
Added splashes were made
With the guard getting soaked
(Between ducks)

A socialite jerk
Fell in love with the "work"
And bought it
For two thousand bucks!

# SPOUSAL DIRGE

Since he has retired
Permit me to say
I've twice as much husband
At half as much pay!

# The Book of Geronimina

4:13

OR: S-S-S-STARTING WITH A B-B-B-BANG

W - W- W - W - WOW!

Had stuttered speaking
Slowed her down
Some might have thought her sickly
But Lo, the lady
Closed the gap
Because she stuttered quickly

# New Apparel Attachments Decried As Pain Inducers

C: 2011 – Dr. Ron Pataky ---- Custom-Ransom-Notes.com

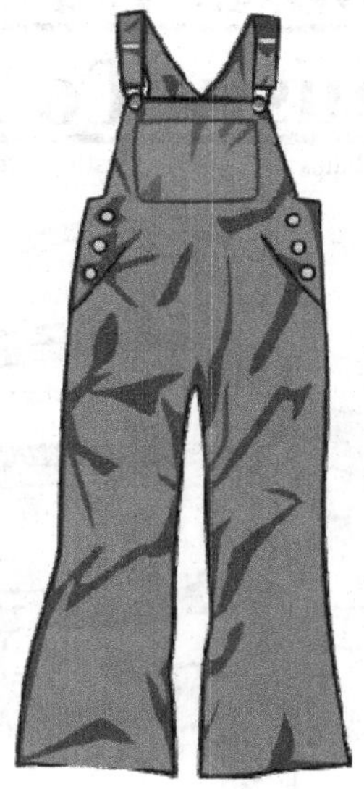

**One considerate maker has them out on top!**

The clothing scene
Can be quite mean
Including countless blunders
These new things ride
AGAINST your hide
Beware, then, of
SUSPUNDERS!

# Six-Year-Old Scholar Looks Back Studiously To Age 3

The last two toes
Of the human foot
Must surely be a joke!
When first (at three!)
They looked at me
My water almost broke!

# Teen 'Lure' Borders On Sheer Madness For One Ex-Bopper!

If you've ever been a teen
You will know just what I mean
When I say that teeny-bopping wasn't easy

As the summers dawdled on
Teenies moped from dusk to dawn
With an attitude that bordered on the queasy

The mornings weren't much
But the evenings really sucked
As we stood around the campus on the preen

And I'm quick to tell you, brothers
If my flabbys had their druthers
I would never, ever, EVER be a teen!

# Chaffeur Insults Termination Results Squire Consults

C: 2011 – Dr. Ron Pataky ---- Cutom-Ransom-Notes.com

SADIE waves bye-bye

The Squire inquired
Why the driver was fired
(EXEMPTING his fling with our Sadie)
The story was short
That his job did abort
When he up and offended THE LADY
Said THE LADY to Daisy
"He's driving me crazy!"
(Thus keeping the umbrage alive)
Said the chauffeur in wait
(Thus sealing his fate!)
"You can tell her it's quite a short drive!"

# Behold the Humble Roll
# Cinnamon, Sesame, or Toilet



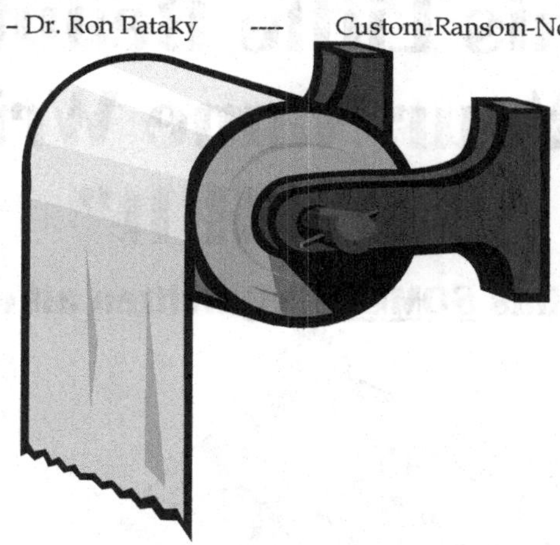

A roll is a thing
You can do on the ground
Or a bun shaped for burgers
Or twisted or round

There's a roll of wax paper
To safeguard your lunch
You can roll up your britches
Or roll with a punch

On a roll while your gambling
Can sweeten your fling
There's no doubt a roll's
A splendiferous thing!

# “This Little Beauty Has Your Name Written All OVER It”

**(Well, it has <u>SOMETHING</u> written all over it!)**

**You know the old saying**
**You’ve heard it in bars**
**When life gives you lemons**

**INSTALL ‘EM IN CARS!!**

<u>MARINARA WARNING</u>

# Keeping Mum Your Only Assurance Against Eventual Gungadin-aling*

You <u>MAY</u> remain quiet!
(The judges have voted!)
Lest later your comments
Have fenced you!

But if you <u>do</u> blabber
You <u>will</u> be misquoted
And every damned quote
Used against you!

*** Bulgarian word meaning 'chicken fat'**

# On the <u>other</u> hand I gotta remember... she's non-refundable!



Nuthin rimes with mabel sue
Least durned if I been abel to
i tried and tried to rite this stuff
An startin now ive had enuf

So if I caint
I tell you true
I gotta dump
Ol mabel sue!

# IMPORTED Models Can Be Tough As Well!

Where pups are concerned
I opt for the mixed
(They seem to have
Much kinder hearts)

There is, though, a catch:
When the puppies need fixed
It's hard to get
MIXED-puppy parts!!

# SILLY CLAUDE

## "The Winner"

**1965-2005**
**(Age 40)**

The silly jackass
Raced through life
As if by demons cursed
And wouldn't you know
Despite the strife
The bastard finished first!

# "It's Like Chattin' With A Bloody Doorknob!"

C: 2011 - Dr. Ron Pataky ---- Custom-Ransom-Notes.com

SHE: "Are you GOING
To that stupid convention??"
HE: (keeps on sippin' his tea)
"The trouble with YOU
Is you don't pay attention!"
HE: "Are you talkin' to me?"

# TURNS OUT THIS BROTHER DIDN'T EVEN WEAR GLASSES!

A sisterly parrot
Hopped into a bar
(Her brother was late for his classes)
Asked the bartender's mother
With thoughts of the brother
"Is he a real tall guy with glasses?"

# Critic Claims Chewier Slop Might Eliminate Need for Mop!

**A brackish Chinese diner**
**Claimed that no food could be finer**
**To which one hardened critic**
**Stated "Phooey"**
**"What you really get's a slop**
**That much more befits a mop!**
**The thing <u>they</u> need's**
**To make their slop more chewy!**

# One Singular DIS-Advantage
# To Pre-Actual-Verbal Prescience

AND ... she was a mere sip away
from actually verbalizing even more!!

**<u>HE</u>:**

I know what you're going
To say e're you say it
(But please, my dear
Don't fear that!)

<u>She</u> paused for a while
Then said with a smile
"I'm sorry you had
To hear that!"

# ONE REALLY, REALLY WICKED SOBRIETY TEST!

With pebbles and gourds (and to justify swords)
A juggler showed coppers his act
The coppers (in awe) almost instantly saw
That his juggling was truly a fact
Two drunks from afar - passing by in a car
Saw the juggler out doing his stuff
Said one to the other
"Damn! Lookee there, brother!
Those road tests are sure getting' tough!!"

# It's Why Minnesota Generally Vanishes In Winter!

Folks from Finland, most agree
Are very much like you and me
They eat and drink and grow their herbs
And conjugate irregular verbs

But Swedes, alas, as most folks know
Cannot be seen against the snow
And that's why winter's statehood quota
Often EXCLUDES Minnesota!

# Multiple Shares Nifty Plan For Painless Waiting

An MPD
Named Pete (times 3)
Kept plans upon a shelf
Each time a date
Would show up late
He'd talk among himself

pssst pssst

NO ... YOU'VE GOT TO BE KIDDING!

# Time's Renovation
# RARELY a Thing of Beauty

Missus or Mizz
Each time you feel'er
You see there are signs
Of attrition
Though time maybe is
A magnificent healer
It's certainly NOT
A beautician!

# THE BOYFRIEND

He now-and-then rocks
But his clothes are a sight!
He's strong as an ox
And almost as bright

# <u>Man Experiences Horrific Comeuppance Via Miffed Missus</u>

**NOTE TONGUE!!**

Bertram – on the whole,
mending middlingly well!

Brutish Bert, mean to the core
Would thump his wife till she was sore
<u>HER</u> goal as she arose each day:
To make the rotten bastard pay!

There came a night [as Bertram snored]
She nailed his privates to a board
And then [egged on by Bertram's bender]
Trundled out the tongue extender

**(OUCH!!)**

# This Year She's Throwing Caution to the Wind!

Two timid fish
In a small bowl resided
Said one, "I am pumped with elation

"I've conquered my fear
And I'm going this year
Clear over there on vacation!"

NOW WHERE'D THE OTHER ONE GO??

# What He REALLY Wanted Was Fresh Mule Eggs!

MULE EGG

MOTHER MULE

The doc gave him horse pills
Which puzzled him greatly
Yet knowing
They must run their courses

With no thought of bills
He planted them straightly
And DID raise
Some pretty neat horses!

# Senator Considers Confusion
## The Staff-Stuff of Life!

Making stuff clear
Is the thing that I fear!
Lest logic turn into a flood!

And it's thusly I pray
Whether yon or today
That no one will water
The mud!

# My Pussycat, However Seems Slightly Mildewed!

C: 2011 - Dr. Ron Pataky --- Custom-Ransom-Notes.com

**~~ QUESTION ~~**

What is the size
Of a waterbed leak?
(We sometimes learn things as we sleep!)

**~~ ANSWER ~~**

The floor to the walls
And the cat to his balls
And a bit more than four inches deep!

# Hey!! Guys "PREFER" What's Available!

There are, of course, exceptions!

Blonde of brunette
Redhead or bald
There's one thing on which
You can bet
What they "PREFER"
Is boy-cow manure
As MOST will take what
They can get!

# At One Time ... Maybe But DON'T Look for Her Where She Was!

To pass the quiz
And prove she is
She wrote her name in paint
Did it behoove her?
Paint remover?
Well, she DID (and ain't!)

# Miss Hyacinth's Confessions Finally Closed Book On Most of Planet's Known Crimes!

Judge Martha Vineyard led the proceedings

Hyacinth Blessing
Was prone to confessing
With countless transgressions
Unfurled

There were from her sessions
(And after confessions)
But three unsolved crimes
In the world!

(And she was suspected of those!)

# FACT: All That Shimmers Is Not Necessarily Crankcase!

I started with nothing
No goodies at all
Disheveled ... completely bereft!

And I found, thinking back
As I wandered the mall
That I still have the bulk
Of it left!

# Bootes & Straddles

Our Senator Bootes
Just INFLATES in his suits!
A windbag of hot air
And prattle
Whether past tense or hence
He has not MET the fence
That he somehow (with time)
Couldn't straddle!

# "What the Heck" Comments Co-Conspirator "Let's Flip a Coin"

"Storing" pathetic wretch until the Big Day!

One haughty peer
In riot gear
To try rebellion cures
Inquired aloud
(To spook the crowd)
"My guillotine or yours?"

# 100th Birthday Memo from Jail

Remember twenty years ago
When we were only eighty?
With pregnancies and STDs
Our worldly woes were weighty

You may recall the time I paged
When all our grit was tested
I'd fussed around with under-aged
And finally got arrested

Two years apart was just a start
When Bubba was released
Because I didn't give a fart
My sentence was increased!

That brought us up to eighty-five
The year we had our Freddy
And then the pall, with cops and all
Which left my days unsteady

And here we're at the century mark
And I'm about to shout
We'll pick it up right where we were
The moment that I'm out!

RECOMMENDED

**AMC**

**American Medical Conglomeration**

# Suggestions For A Pre-Surgery Chat With Your Docter

While I'm still awake
Take care, goodness sake
From incision at first, then to suture

I pray while you're numbing
Take care of my plumbing
I'd like to be there for my future!

# A Few Parsley Potatoes And She'd Positively Swoon!

A fricasseed flounder
Liked trimmings around her
Like garlic, verbena, and thyme
And always a kind
Of a small citrus rind
(And when joyously festive, a lime!)

# They TRIED to Keep It Hushed But, Alas, It Leaked Out!

Chief Naka-Jo-Wee
Drank gallons of tea
He drank and he drank
Until sleepy
And it wasn't the rain
Nor a leak in the drain
That drowned him that night
In his tea-pee!

# Alternating & Intermittent Gap Flaps Result In Bum Raps For Gaps



THIS
IS
A GAP!

>>> GAP <<<

Some Gappings give pause
Though they're there for a cause
And gaps often get a bum rap
Some gripe if any!
And some if too many!
And some whisper

"Pssssst ... What's a gap?"

# Folks in the South Simply More Genteel!



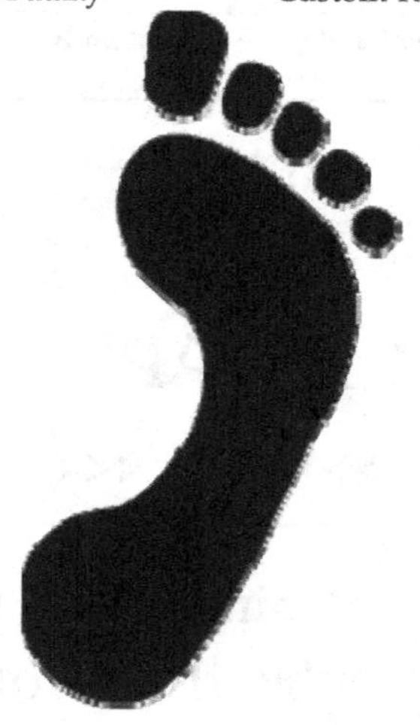

For folks in the South
It is graciously put:
A firmly closed mouth
Gathers no foot!

# NOTICE !
# FROM GARIBALDI !

## New Cult Wants Everything You Have!
## Will Share Everything THEY Have
## If & When They Have Anything!



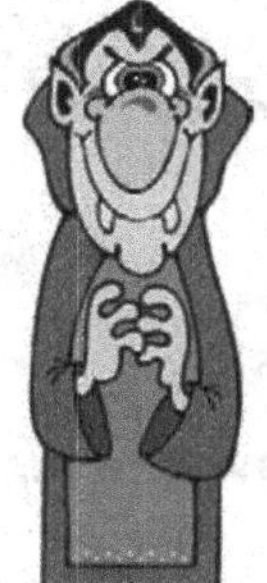

Mighty Exalted, Most Glorified Bishop Garibaldi

Come ye child or adult
I am starting a cult
You'll adore our new
Stiff, starchy collars
For the meeting of ends
Kindly round up eight friends
Who will EACH send me
Ten thousand dollars!

# Slice-of-Life Segment From First Trip To Switzerland



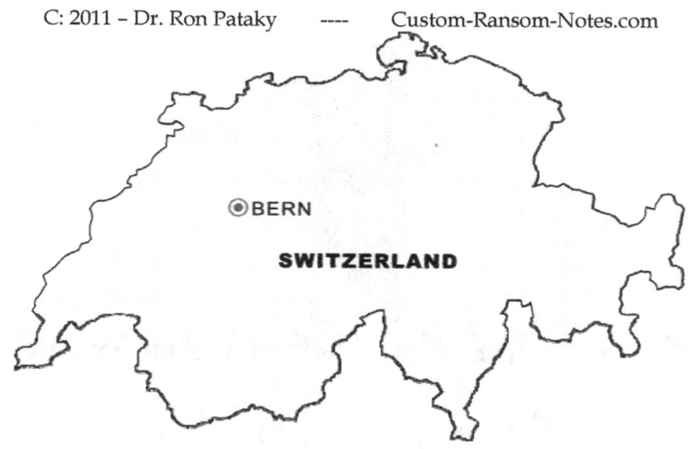


"I gave the beggar
Fifty bucks
That's more than forty francs!"

"What on earth
Did your husband say?"

"YOU KIDDIN'?
HE SAID 'THANKS'!"

# The Colorful Afternoon The Gay Pirates Swooped Us

The pirates were everywhere
Swirling their nets
And swishing aboard
Using sails
A few flashing swords
Dangling FABULOUS cords!
And two or three
Buffing their nails

# HUMONGOUS SOLUTION



● ● ● ● ●

The rain was fierce
A sticky goo
And I alone
Knew what to do

I drilled some holes
(So folks could live)
And made the earth
A giant sieve!

**PARENTS:**

**YOU MAY WANT TO POST THIS ON YOUR FRIDGE**

# GET READY, SUBURBIA WE'RE GONNA HAVE A GIANT SPOTTED SALE!

Worse yet, 50,000 spotted ties came with them!

It's right there on their manifests
A hundred million spotted vests!
To sell (or else the store is gonna fail!)

There is a way to skip the fights
To hell with pots and pans and whites
We're gonna have a

**MONSTER <u>SPOTTED</u> SALE!**

# There Were Other Things But Her Bodacious Curves REALLY Zonked Him!

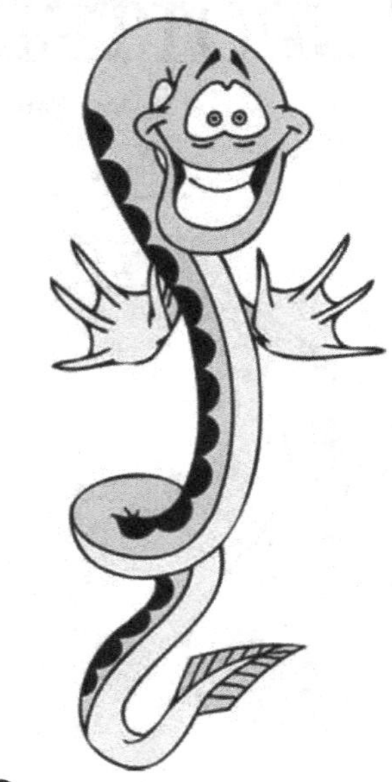

Oooooooo - weeeeee!

The gorgeous girl-snake
Slithered by
With typical feminine tact
Exclaimed the guy-snake
Standing by
"OH WOW!
THAT BABE IS STACKED!"

# Fern Fends Off Gnats In Sticky Farm Offensive

**Her pathetic option was *8,283* messy executions per day!**

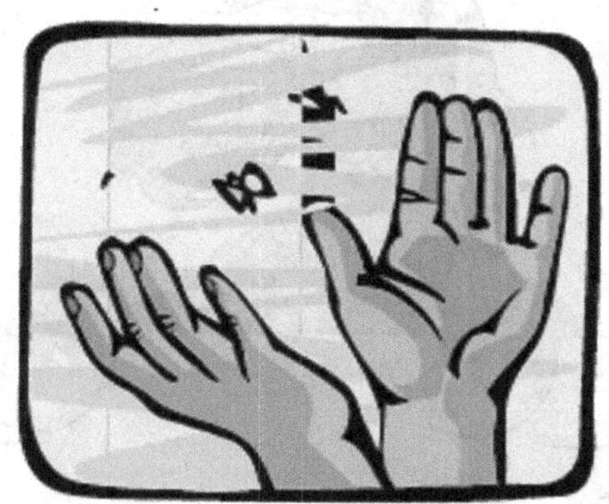



Fern had a farm
On which she raised beans
But she hated bean-gnats
In the halls
So she scraped up the means
For re-patching the screens
Then she quickly gnat-papered
The walls!

Stay Tuned, Nature Lovers!

# Coming Soon to our Site: Great SOUNDS of Nature!

"Don't you dare miss this'n!"
says Charlie

"Great Smells of Nature"
Is now on our site
For patrons who fancy
A whiff
One lousy buck
Gets your fanny unstuck
Then you go to your door
And you sniff!

# Pulverized Chips, Rancid Dip Didn't Help The Case, Either!

Sure LOOKS like Cousin Phil, doesn't it?

Ground meat had been found
Two feet down in the ground
In the rain a quite drizzly recovery
When the meat spoiling there
Turned out to be bear
They called it "a grizzly discovery"

# Check of Family Tree Yields Startling Granny News!

The tree didn't do all that well, either!

I checked my family tree
With glee
But not all facts have jived
My great-great grandma
Had twelve kids
And not a one survived!

# Bulkier Spikes, Slivers, or Splinters
# Would SOMETIMES
# Gum the Works!



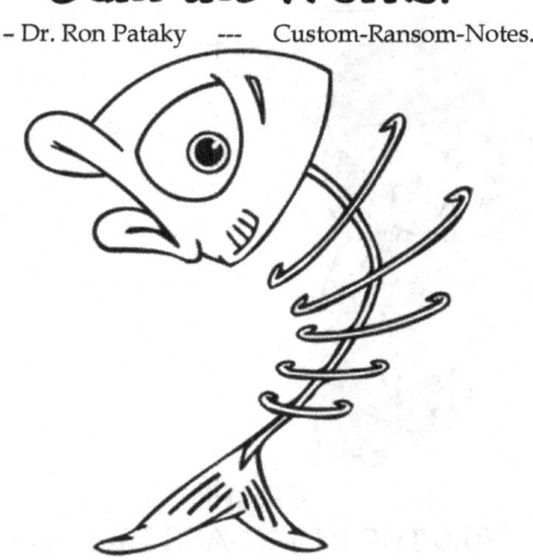

Cyrus Jones
Had spindly bones
And hence this lack-of-couth trick

All supper long
He'd flake a prong
And use it as a toothpick

# Okay, You Artsy-Fartsy Dudes & Chicks... YOUR Day Is Coming!!

CRAP!!
ALL THE DUMB-ASS BROADS
ARE SCRIBBLED ON!!

In fifty-some years
And despite all the tears
And WHATEVER retirement
You choose
You will find in the gloom
Of the huge common room
You're surrounded
By wrinkled tattoos!

# News Of Test Pilot Lock-Out Startles Scientists

The test pilot's hop
To the atmosphere top
(Where no human ever had been)
Shot him right through the roof
Where (no longer aloof)
He found he could not get back in!!

# Gee, Honey, Are We Having A Good Time Yet??

A nasty summer lightning storm, you say?
PERFECT !

Hotdogs to fill
A rusty old grill
And dog-buns as old as they seem
Throw in stale Fritos
And lots of mosquitoes
And that's the American dream!

**Applied Inverse Proportionality**

# Balthazar's 1st Law Of Knowledge Acquisition

**The more you know**
**The less you don't know**

**(Will write when I know more!)**

## ACCIDENT SUMMARY

# Tests Show Train Engineer Goozled Tee Miny Martoonies

**After Murphy imbibed**
**Many folks were described**
**In various brittle**
**And fried ways**
**His train arrived late**
**Tracks ELEVEN <u>through</u> EIGHT**
**As it rammed the old depot-dock**
**SIDEWAYS!**

# From Ancient Cornucopian Tablets

Sayings are true
If they ring true to you
And truth is true
Whither thou goest!

He who laughs last
May indeed laugh best
But he who laughs last's
Also slowest!

Cornucopia
1626

# Picture, If You Can, Late News By Flame!

Standard or metric
Thank God for electric
(As we're sitting there
In our sandals)

Imagine the scene
With no lamplight to glean:
We would have to watch shows
Using candles!

# Pole Count



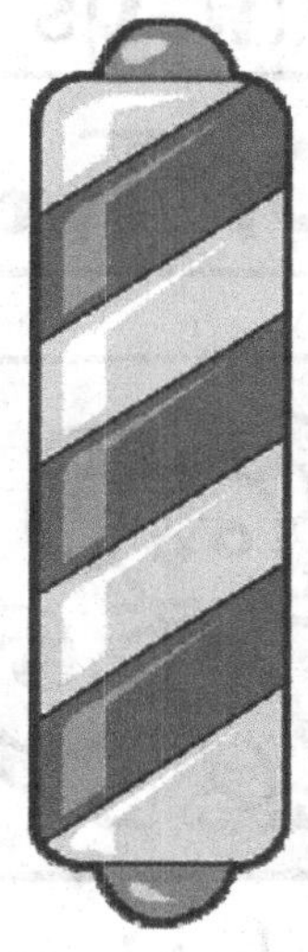

To see's long been
Among my goals
The Czechs abundant
As the Poles

For even if
He's not one
Every barber's
Got one

# And If NOT There's Always A Dipper Or Two!

A rodent in space
Was seeking a place
And one day was told
By a mole
"If you're willing to chance her
We may have the answer
My wife THINKS she's found
A black hole"

# Y'all Know ... One 'a Them Once-In-A-Lifetime Experiences!

Only a tattered photo remains!

Said the blind clarinetist
Of Earth's flaming core
"It's quite unlike anything
I've seen before!

Then said he, emerging
From blaze there within
"And I really don't reckon
I'll see it again!"

# I Tell You, Officer You're Not Making Any Sense At All!

"Your license, my dear
There's a speed limit here
And you are expected
To go it!"

"It was just yesterday
That you took it away
And now you expect me
To show it?"

# Blizzard Notes

**DEAR DIARY**

**Snow while sleep**
**Mighty deep**
**[Found when we had poled it]**
**'Cross the grounds**
**A MILLION pounds!**
**Hope the ground can hold it!**

TRAVEL NEWS: IFFYSTAN

# Then There's Iffystan Where Some Do & Some Don't!

C: 2011 - Dr. Ron Pataky --- Custom-Ransom-Notes.com

In Zanadoo
Do monkeys poo
So tourists say they
Won't

Go there at all
But to Nepal
Where PROPER monkeys
Don't!

COOKING CLASS

# And for a Pert Dessert We Recommend The Sassy Plung

A classic Sassy Plung ... with boogyberries!

Consider the Radish
A glorious thing
Eclipsing the sweet Rutabaga
And if in your planting
You fancy a fling
Consider the luscious Tomega
But jumping out front
As we water our plots
Is the already sacrosanct "BLIBBLE"
Described by my aunt
As a six-legged plant
That many are starting to nibble!

MOTHER GROUSE RHYMES

# In Fact, The NAUGHTY Pirates Spent a LOT of Time Behind It!

A pirate in wait
Kept a HUGE ball of eight
For buying new slaves
Near the gate wall
When these mongers of hate
Would ask, "Where is my mate?"
He would tell 'em
"They're all over there
Behind building fourteen"

# Illusive Furry Fleas Lead To Zanzibaran Snookie

Common possum actually observing Zanzibaran Snookie

Mergatroyd (despite his fears)
Had searched the jungle many years
(Though many thought
His expeditions kooky)

He scraped the droppings, if you please
For speckled mites and furry fleas
The foodstuff
Of the Zanzibaran Snookie

# Maturity Takes a Bit Longer In Some Than It Does In Others!

Timothy Ruff
Was street-knocker tough
A bruiser with plugs ever-revvin'

Said a chum "Yea, it's kicks
But you are only six.
For goodness sakes
Wait till you're seven."

# When In Doubt, Sherlock

# ASK A CRO-MAGNON!!

Fred: Warming up for the ochre exhibit

So what are YOUR thoughts
On the human race?
I asked a mob boss and his minion
Then I pointedly fed
The question to Fred
As I sought an outsider's opinion

# Which Part of Under Don’t You Stand?

C: 2011 – Dr. Ron Pataky --- Custom-Ransom-Notes.com

SHE says HE nibbles
But HE says SHE quibbles
And that is the crux of their troubles

While he claims her quibblings
Concerning his nibblings
Are NOT merely innocent flubbles

“Oh, his flubble’s trouble!
Oh, yeah, make that double!”
She screams (although NOT without giggling)

“Well, poo on her rue
I have better to do
And I tell you HER quibblings are niggling!”

**FINALLY!**
**OLAF'S VERY FIRST CONCERT IN ENGLISH**

# YANK My doodle It's a Dandy...

# Examining the Convergence Of Young Females and Zits

Tell him I'm pontooning in Madagascar!

Reading in Flemish
A pimple is "blemish"
You use a Dutch "B" and that's it
In Turkeyshoot Junction
It's "Facial Malfunction"
But everywhere else it's a ZIT!
You can buy some creams
(Oh yeah, right! In your dreams!)
That promise a night to be kissed
But here's how it plays
It will be there for days!!
**(AND YOUR DATE**
**WILL JUST HAVE TO BE PISSED!!)**

<u>NEXT WEEK</u>:

# Why One-Legged Monkeys Walk With A Bounce!

Consider the case
Of the one-legged duck:
Whether prosthesis'll work'll
Determine in time
If the duck (with some luck!)
Can stop swimming round
In a circle !

# And, After It's Over I REALLY Need A Nap!

Picking on procrastinators
Is my favorite sport
But in each rhyme
There comes a time
At which I must abort

The problem is this thing I've got
To which I always cater
With mind a blot
And springs all shot
I plan to do it later

# What Can We Say? It's What Happens When The Year of the Mongooses Converges With A Limp & Iffy Solstice!

Nineteen days hath September
April, June, and November
All the remainder
Now have thirty-six
And those are the months
That we're trying to fix

# A Simpler Time

My Christmas gift
Long years ago:
A crooked stick
Which I could throw

My favorite thing
I do believe
Was first to toss
And then retrieve!

I still can see it
'though it's hard
That damp and smelly
Vacant yard

To moan and piss
Is not my kick
But how I miss
That crooked stick!

# Reward for Her Capture: Fifty Thousand Forested Acres!

An arsonist named Mother Nature's
Lurking hereabout
With sparking clout
Without the route of wires!

She often works us while we sleep
(Though days are not ruled out)
As she leaps around the planet
Setting fires!

# GREETINGS!

## Inus Usum Weebit

*"There's a little bit of ourselves in each of us!"*



## SECTION TWO

## Indisspensable Lessons Re: Little-Known History

(Followed by more life-changing rhymes!)

Thanks ... and enjoy!
And always keep foremost in mind:

HE WHO SO SHALL
SO THEN SHALL HE WHO!

# THE MOST COLORFUL CONDUCTOR OF THEM ALL

The late Arturo Toscanini, whose vituperative tongue-lashings withered many a cummerbund during his long and tempestuous musical career, seems to have been uncharacteristically tractable when it came to a question much bandied by musicologists during the mid-1950s: specifically, who was the most colorful conductor of all time?

Indeed, just prior to his death in 1957, the volatile Toscanini, not exactly a vapid maestro in his own right, sent major shock waves throughout the entire musical world by suggesting that the elusive distinction might well have belonged to a man not only virtually unknown to the world at large, but also, incredibly enough, not even conservatory-trained! It was an utterance that served to stagger musicologists everywhere, particularly coming from the cantankerous Toscanini, whose fearsome pursuit of perfection was legendary.

The maestro freely admitted that he had never actually witnessed a performance by the man in question, and that his opinion, while unyielding, was nonetheless based on pure hearsay. He insisted, however (to the dyspeptic chagrin of countless pretenders to the would-be throne), that it was hearsay of a most reliable nature. Typically, to the very moment of his death, Toscanini clung tenaciously to his firm and provocative contention, producing even more enemies among his contemporaries than might otherwise have been the unenviable norm.

According to the maestro, the distinction of the most colorful conductor of all time belonged (and no doubt still belongs) to an obscure traveling purveyor of lightning rods, who, in the course of plying his humble wares through western Kansas in 1929, inadvertently became a kind of instant folk hero --- of such legendary stature, in fact, that his very name continues to this day to be spoken in hushed, reverent tones by the common folk of the region.

(Nor, for what it is worth, does the narrative appear in the least to be merely another tall, Bunyonesque tale designed to cajole well-heeled passers-by into blithely converting their short-term cash into long-term memorabilia. As new world tragedies go, this one, according to no less an authority than the late Homer Gigslapp, rivaled Hiawatha itself for sheer, soul-numbing pathos).

The man's name was Ferd Dumpster -- as mentioned, a lightning-rod salesman by trade.

The story goes that Dumpster was walking across a wheat field with an armload of samples one sultry August afternoon in 1929, taking what was obviously a short cut from the Peabody place to Buck McSpoon's spread. As fate would have it, his momentarily peaceful stroll just happened to coincide with the arrival of what old-timers agreed was easily the most intense and thoroughly formidable electrical storm to pass that way in a century or more.

And so it was that Ferd Dumpster made his memorable

debut. Struck quite suddenly by some sort of thitherto unknown ability, the man that day delivered a performance that was, in the opinion of witnesses as far as seven fields away, positively glowing. Several thought they recognized a little-known Aaron Copeland composition in Dumpster's wildly-flailing shoulder gestures and the erratic rhythmic structure of his overall florid histrionics. Two dissenters, however, suspected by more than a few of being Russian spies, rather tipped the scales by arguing that the work was undeniably Shostakovich. Which, if either, of the opinions was correct is a question to which we may, alas, never have an answer?

The performance lasted nearly eight minutes in all, and certainly, if the aforementioned witnesses can be believed, ranked with the most vivid and animated of all time. Indeed, it was the unanimous testimony of these very witnesses that convinced Toscanini of Dumpster's credentials concerning the title of (in the words of Toscanini himself) "the ultimate conductor." Coming from the maestro, it was in any event the ultimate compliment.

The argument concerning which composer Dumpster was interpreting that impulsive afternoon rages on to the present day throughout most of western Kansas, although the truth, once again, probably will never be known. Sadly, this was the one and only performance of Dumpster's brief but brilliant career, the man having collapsed immediately after his final bow into a coma from which he never recovered.

Some have endeavored to mollify the tragedy by pointing out that the sheer Herculean energy depleted in his performance probably precluded the question of an encore in any event. This, however, undoubtedly was of little comfort to those whose artistic souls he touched so deeply that memorable day.

Whatever the case, most were in agreement that it was an incredible sequence of disastrous events to befall a man who was not even a Biblical character, and it was in the immediate wrenching aftermath that noted folk poet A. L. "Gus" Whipside composed his famous ode, known to school children everywhere and concluding with those immortal lines:

***"The good may die young and importune,***
***but the truly electrified***
***more-oft go immediately"***

Dumpster is buried in the historic Lonesome Gloam Cemetery, about 15 miles west of Bushwhacker, Kansas, where his grave marker, artistically fashioned from his beloved lightning rods, receives the frequent attention of man and nature alike. Some in the area steadfastly claim that his ghost can occasionally be seen twitching and cavorting across the plains during the area's many violent summer storms. This, however, is completely undocumented, and probably amounts to little more than traditional wheat field superstition, birthed along the way somehow by an unknown prairie bloat, and sustained thereafter by a blurred sea of pathetically marblized Oddlyballs.

# THE BALLAD OF HARRY JEMIMA

## An Utterly Almost-True Short Story

 Custom-Ransom-Notes.com

The unique half-century-plus saga of a quaint burger and fries operation in the tiny village of Woodchuck, Wyoming (pop. 393, and the county seat despite its small size), was undoubtedly less awesome than the phenomenal success in recent decades of such as McDonald's and Wendy's. In most ways, however, it was indisputably more colorful.

Hairless Harry's, an institution in Woodchuck from its founding amidst the very height of the depression until the sad and untimely death of its popular owner in 1996, was a seven-stool, four-table emporium whose grill was first fired up in the fall of 1931 by an even then toothless cherub of a man named Harry Jemima.

Although connected in no way with the famous waffle and pancake lady, Harry was dubbed Uncle Jemima almost from the beginning by the local kids. It was an affectionate name he would carry for nearly seven decades, during which time he served as friend, father confessor, cholesterol donor, and all-round good-guy counselor to generations of youngsters growing up during those carefree years in the sandlots and back roads of scenic Woodchuck.

Although Hairless Harry's proved a place of assembly for all young folks, boys in particular seemed drawn to the humble roadside shack, undaunted by its patched screen door, peeling wallpaper, and ever-present gnats and flies. Always inexplicably polite when around Harry, they came in mini-droves --- lunchtime, after school, and weekends during the school year, and from dawn until closing during the cool and pleasant summers. They came to eat, of course. Mostly, however, they came to talk for hours on end concerning the perennial topics of teens everywhere --- sports, music, touted pimple cures, unsympathetic parents, unconscionable teachers, hotrods...and girls.

As one might guess, the "hairless" in his perhaps inevitable appellative was the result of the utterly obvious fact that that Harold Walter Franklin Jemima III had not so much as a single wisp of hair on his visible body (indeed, one can only marvel at the speculation that must have gone on during those years - boys being boys - concerning what secrets the *covered* portions of his dough-like frame might hold).

In any event, the off-hand remark of one young wag (who went on to author his own weekly column for the Daily Bugle in nearby Tungsten) summed it up for most. "Forget all of the baldness analogies you've ever heard," the budding humorist observed, "Uncle Jemima's head makes a billiard ball look positively unkempt."

Harry Jemima's untimely death in 1996 came as an indirect result of his near-lifelong penchant for nibbling bird gravel, a habit dating back to his early teens when he'd first discovered the delights of pigeon-breeding. As some children develop a bizarre fondness for consuming dirt - as some farmers get absolutely hooked on munching field corn or alfalfa - so it was that Harry cultivated his long-standing predilection for bird gravel.

Suffice it to say, since he was still inordinately robust at the time of his death at age 89, the ingestion of coarse bits of battered stone over the years had not affected his health in the least. In more ways than one, Harry Jemima was a vivid and memorable specimen.

His unfortunate demise was set in motion the morning he made the decision to close shop for the first Saturday ever in order to attend the annual ***Knights of Sequatchie*** picnic, held each September at the nearby reservoir, where real linen tablecloths and attractive stone grills gave the annual event an undeniable aura of big-city finery.

His decision was sealed when he learned that dessert on that pleasant autumn day would consist of individual honey-bran loaves absolutely awash in his favorite gooseberry preserves, "put up" only days before by the good ladies of the Woodchuck Quilting Society. At the same time, he was smitten by the last-minute announcement that later in the evening an Italian fellow all the way from Boise would render musical selections in a back-lit "silhouette" mandolin concert from behind a genuine Venetian silk screen. It was by all odds the social event of the season, and Harry, in a moment of uncharacteristic abandon, was coaxed into taking a quick swim (fully clothed, of course) with the rest of the gang, most of whom (not, as it turned out, that it would have mattered) were many times his junior.

For Harry, the "swim" lasted only slightly longer than it takes an anvil to hit the bottom of a hot tub. Indeed, loaded down as usual with the ballast of the bird gravel he had consumed throughout the morning, he exhibited all the flotation qualities of a granite boulder, sinking like a veritable shot to the slippery bottom of an area estimated to be 25 feet deep. It was only after a dozen or so volunteer divers had spent nearly an hour determining that they could not so much as budge his now-enormous weight that a construction crane was summoned from a bridge construction site in the next county. Alas, to no one's surprise, it was by that time simply too late.

The sun was well down as the crane arrived on the scene and managed to hoist the gravel-laden body from the deep, ripping off an entire historic dock as it swung ponderously to the shoreline. Harry was pronounced dead at precisely 8:51 p.m. by T. Crockett Murfle, a taxidermist from nearby Clover Hollow and the only person present even remotely qualified to officiate at the unhappy occasion. It was to a silent and disheartened assemblage that Taxidermist Murfle finally made his expected announcement.

Harry's funeral, needless to say, was a thoroughly emotional affair, as ex-students came from far and wide to join present-day residents in a procession that exceeded by at least double Woodchuck's full three-block distance between "Welcome to Woodchuck" and "Visit us again!" All present that glorious September afternoon were solemnly hushed as Harry's body, apron-clad and virtually smothered in brilliant autumn leaves, was carted to the nearby cemetery, the hand-beveled chestnut casket riding in the bed of Harry's familiar azure panel truck, its sides cut away for the occasion. Sadly emblazoned in bright crimson script on each rusted door was "Eat at Hairless Harry's." At the cemetery, Pastor Wilbur Nufterborg of the First Baptist Church read words over him.

The much-loved Harry Jemima, a man whose glistening pate would make a billiard ball "look positively unkempt," was gone forever. Ceremoniously buried with him were his beloved spatula, a quart crock of his favorite gravel, a yellowed photo depicting his grand opening back in 1931, and the worn latchkey to Hairless Harry's.

It would, of course, never open again.

# THE CURSE OF A LESS-THAN-HONEST FACE

C: 2011 – Dr. Ron Pataky ---- Custom-Ransom-Notes.com

(Facsimile)

Colonel Beauregard Bartholomew Pew III, whose cavalier swashbuckling has both shocked and delighted the citizens of Washburn, Kentucky, for longer than most could remember, is a man whose career should have gone much, much further than it did. Indeed, as most folks in the white-fenced bluegrass community would vouch, few men anywhere could match Colonel Beau's rare amalgam of wealth, prestige, lineage, wit, and charm.

For 70 years and more, however, Beau B. Pew III has been burdened by a defect of sorts, unrecognized through the decades by those around him who had, so to speak, grown accustomed to his face. Simply put, Beau Pew had (and continues to have) a decidedly dishonest look about him. Throughout his lifetime, he just did not, by any stretch of fancy, give off the reassuring glow of a man in whom one could reasonably have even nominal faith.

As long as he stayed in his own community, things were fine. When venturing among strangers, however, the rope of survival inevitably slickened, as the good Colonel's luckless facial features invariably created an aura of suspicion and distrust. It was just that kind of face.

When traveling, for instance, it was not uncommon for the Colonel, despite always being immaculately groomed, to pay cash for a purchase and still be asked for identification; or, for a perfect stranger to approach him (exactly as one recently did in Atlanta), and mumble something on the order of "aren't you the SOB who sold me that lousy Studebaker?"

Particularly distressing to Colonel Pew were those not infrequent occasions when, for example, a saleslady not known to him would nervously say something like "I'm not sure we have enough cash on hand to change a five," her voice trailing off as she frantically (and obviously), scouted the terrain to see if there might be a policeman nearby.

It was, as we've said, just that kind of face.

The sad part was the fact that, despite the success and excellent name he enjoyed in his home community, it had always been Beau's heartfelt desire to someday enter statewide politics. (It was a dream that went as far back as second grade, when a noble elementary teacher named Miss Clickers had given him his first straight-up academic dose of Civics).

Even as a straight "A" student in both junior and senior high, young Beau would routinely forsake Friday night games and sweaty sock-hops to withdraw instead into the latest book on politics or politicians. Biographies were his favorite, the Civil War his specialty, and Robert E. Lee, Jefferson Davis, and General Horatio Sideburn his lifelong idols.

Young Beau had no illusions about becoming governor or anything like that; not even lieutenant governor necessarily. It was just that he doted on the notion of running for political office. Any office. And while he didn't exactly reek of self-confidence as a youth, he was not completely lacking in it either. This, of course, was before his eventual curdling realization that distrust was as inevitable as Monday morning, given...well, just given the way he looked.

As he dejectedly discovered by his early twenties, his face was too blatantly dishonest even for politics. After the single try he ever made for public office - in September of 1943 - he jarringly concluded that absolutely no one who didn't know him personally would <u>ever</u> vote for a face like his. His campaign slogan, "vote for the man, not the face," was (perhaps prophetically) of little help. By this time, the problem was apparent to all. In the '43 election, Pew received only 87 votes out of the more than 623,000 cast in the district that day, losing in a rare Kentucky Tsunami to a sniveling racetrack tout named Peaford "Putz" Biglutz. (Things only became worse when Biglutz was suspicious of Pew's 87 votes and demanded a recount!). Only incidentally, it had not helped things at all when Pew completely froze on camera during his first and only televised public debate. Commenting on his opponent's disjointed ramblings, he suddenly stopped short, unable for the life of him to come up with the phrase "mental block."

Nor had it helped either when, mere days before the election, his faithful campaign helper, Gladys Rumdumdekker (no relation to the Venetian gondola refurbisher, Ribbadick Rumdumdekker) had to be rushed into emergency mouth and lingual surgery after carelessly gargling with Adhesive-Release. Gladys, obviously rattled at the time, said she'd been trying, after licking several thousand <u>self</u>-adhering postage stamps by mistake, to emancipate her tongue from her lower lip and squishy side-gums.

Beau was a survivor, however, and faithfully continued to astutely navigate the mud-clumped road of life, eventually graduating from law school and serving a short but fruitful apprenticeship with a prestigious Washburn law firm. Eventually, he emerged cicada-like as a full-fledged and quite expert patent attorney. His financial guerdon continued its exponential flowering, particularly so after the autumn of 1954, when he finally landed the much-coveted Lodestar Chemical account. (They, of course, are the folks who isolated the elusive and recherché kiwi enzyme that would result in the world's supreme shoe polish).

Colonel Beau finally married and, although it took his wife nearly a decade to absolutely believe him when he said something like "I'll be back in half an hour," the marriage, like everything except his face in Beau's life, was a keeper. In 1997, they celebrated their 50th wedding anniversary.

The Pews also are proud owners of two bouncing daughters, Miss Walola and Miss Citronella, who, although quite normal in virtually every respect (they mercifully did not inherit their father's "dishonest" genes), nonetheless remain maiden ladies well into their late-fifties. To be perfectly candid, their continuing single status almost certainly has something to do with the fact that eligible strangers never knew for absolute certain who the girls really were. When a friendly and smiling Beau would say "these are my daughters," no one, of course, actually believed him. So it was and is that they remain more or less social orphans to this day.

Yes, such was and is the magnitude of the cruel joke played by nature on Beau Pew.

Despite the near-blinding aura of distrust his presence continually created, Beau Pew remained and remains to and through his retirement an elegantly honest man. Indeed, the only remotely misleading incidental of his entire life and career was his use of the honorary "Colonel" title on his business cards, a completely accepted practice in that region of the south. And even that he used with unwavering dignity and aplomb.

Beau's retirement in 1989 finally eased things a bit. After a lifetime of unwarranted skepticism on the part of strangers, he could at last float in his thatched rocker, listen dreamily to the mellifluous strains of "My Old Kentucky Home," and, sipping on a cooling julep, not care much one way or the other.

Occasionally, however, not unlike supremely bad dreams and sadly typical boomerangs, the familiar appearance issue returns yet one more time to stain an otherwise spotless moment in time.

Strolling leisurely into his old law office one pristine morning last spring, for example, Beau was surprised and delighted to see a new young face at one of the attorney desks. "Hi there," he said cheerily, extending a firm and friendly hand. "I'm Beau Pew."

"Sure you are, Mac," the stranger growled in reply, "and I'm Queen Isabella."

# ON THE WHOLLY TRANSCENDENT SEDUCTIONS OF CHEESE

Of the dazzling array of foodstuffs known to man throughout the globe, from the fragile and exotic guma guluba fruit of Tierra del Fuego to black Parisian truffles and the rugged roadside rutabaga, no comestible anywhere offers homo sapiens a greater variety of colors, smells, tastes, and textures than does the humble cheese - citizen, if ever there was one, of the world. Nor, few would argue, does the viand exist that permits a broader range of delectable serving possibilities and companion dishes.

Soft or hard, white, yellow, pumpkin, or blue, cheese comes as close as any victual imaginable to being the universal food, consumed almost everywhere in some form, readily metamorphosed from its generally abundant dairy source, and routinely achieving a quality touted by aficionados as perfection itself. Indeed, to borrow a concept from the late Father Flannigan, there seems to be no such thing as a bad cheese. Small wonder, then, that the exquisite spongy curd is taken so much for granted by most of us.

The common dairy cow no doubt comes first to mind when most Americans droolingly contemplate the origin of their cheese of choice; and it is unquestionably true that a disproportionate number of American favorites are lovingly coaxed from the frothy harvest of your basic, garden-variety bovine (with goats running a not-so-close second).

But cheese is made available by other mammals as well, some of which may surprise even acknowledged connoisseurs (defined for our purposes as those who can, without reference, extemporize on why it is that a portion of the whey is always retained in the curd). This group of suitable lactiferous creatures includes sheep, camel, reindeer and elk, water buffalo, moose, llamas, and yaks. (As to the latter, the heady nectar of an extremely stout Himalayan hybrid known as the Wide-Track Yak is reputed to be especially toothsome).

For those societies whose environment is simply too harsh for the domestication of conventional herds, other pathways to cheese have evolved, merely enhancing the popular perception that cheese is indeed the universal food. Where it is not routinely available, man, it would seem, goes about the clever business of *making* it available.

The Eskimos, by way of example, have long produced the wonderfully delectable mukmuk as a staple second only to raw blubber in their daily diet - which, some claim, accounts for the fact that tooth fillings, dentures and braces are virtually unknown among the various remote Eskimo tribes (as, for that matter, are dentists).

A soft, ambrosial confection spawned from the rich and pungent broth of lactating walruses, mukmuk has been consumed throughout the far northern climes for at least 2,000 years, although only in modern times has its existence become known to most outsiders. Indeed, public demand for the zesty walrus cheese has become so widespread in recent years that Nanook's Snow Pit, the four-star Arctic beanery famous for its carved-tusk flatware (with several exquisite patterns long available to blushing Eskimo brides), now features fresh mukmuk right up there with such traditional delicacies as Minced Albatross Pudding, Blubber

Benedict, Candied Caribou, and Tern Liver Pie ("leave no Tern unstoned," local hunters are reminded) among its esteemed "Nuggets of the Day." (Note: the same is now true of Lester's Tundra Inn, which, according to the Eureka Herald, is Alaska's only current <u>five-star</u> eatery).

As with some exceptional wines, the origins and unusual names of even common cheeses frequently are shrouded in mystery. Indeed, also like some fine wines, the secret methods of producing certain cheeses have been kept under lock and key for centuries. With the advent of advanced research techniques and instant worldwide communication, however, some long-standing myths finally are being displaced by fact (frequently losing considerable zest in the process).

Kazakhstan's sublime Gorzonzola is a much-bandied case in point. Legend notwithstanding, the fact is that there never was a huge monster by this name; and certainly not one whose uncontrollable digging habits eons ago turned a once-flat coniferous plain into what today is Italy's lovely Po Valley. (<u>Godzilla</u>, some will recall, was based on this absurd fable).

There also is a certain irony to feta cheese being the unchallenged favorite of Greeks everywhere. Many purists believe Feta's minimum aging time of <u>only four days</u> hardly befits the otherwise magnificent classical heritage passed on to humanity by the splendor that was Ancient Greece. Greeks, of course, call it nitpicking, pointing out that certain Italian red wines, generally accepted without undue fuss, are rendered drinkable in four <u>hours</u>!

The best example of historical misinterpretation, of course, concerns swiss cheese (always with a small "s"), which quite simply is not a product of Switzerland at all. In fact, its original name was <u>swish</u> cheese, born as the result of the exotic acoustical effect generated by the "swishing" of blossom-scented evening breezes through the cheese's many holes as it swung from the rafters of mud huts on the outskirts of Peking, China, where it is believed to have originated. Although history is sketchy at best, multiple early missionaries (Hudson Taylor as one notable example) reported during the early years of the China Inland Mission that their Chinese friends, among whom bells, wind chimes, and sundry gongs were and are considered heirlooms, were the first people anywhere to routinely drill holes in their cheese, undoubtedly seeking to create precisely the pleasurable swishing sound they eventually managed to achieve with such lovely and exotic results.

(Note: to replicate this delightful experience, hang three or four pieces of plain old, store-bought swish cheese outside of your bedroom window on a warm, breezy night. The lulling acoustical effect is guaranteed to ease you into truly magnificent slumber, although a few subjects do report being disturbed in their rest by olfactory notions of pastrami and-or rye bread).

In any event, it was in this way that swish cheese was born, with the incorrect variation familiar to most Americans (i.e. "Swiss," as in Switzerland) apparently having resulted early on from a linguistic peculiarity that renders the Pekinese unable to pronounce the tricky "ss" sound of most western tongues. (The normally-dreaded "eze" sound, as in "cheese," apparently offered no such speech restriction).

Given the countless fascinating cheese peculiarities extant in the world today, space necessarily precludes more thorough treatment here. Serious students, however, are directed to the author's new cinematic work, ***Cheese! the Movie!***, opening at theaters everywhere in the spring of the coming year. Among its numerous startling revelations, it chronicles the sudden and sassy origins of Havarti, the real story of Limburger, the glory that was Gouda, and the shockingly questionable lineage of Lunkenkranzl.

**Watch for**

# CHEESE! THE MOVIE!

# VOILA! AND HENCE A MUSICAL FENCE!



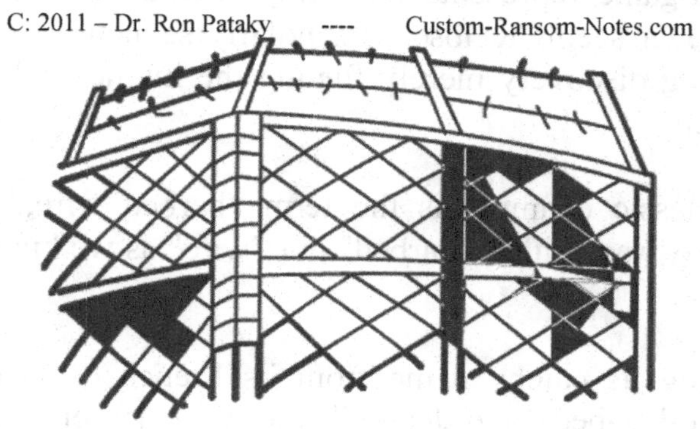

Sooner or later, in one fashion or another, all intelligent writing invariably returns home to roost in the comfortable and familiar branches of etymology, that fascinating field of study dealing with the origins of words and phrases. Indeed, as scholarly endeavors go, etymology ranks without question among the most compelling and absorbing of them all, every jot the equal of such research sweethearts as geneology, medicinal herbs, and bird plumage.

Among the fascinations of etymological research is the frequent delight of discovering words and phrases whose original linguistic purpose bears little or no resemblance to their present usage. The word <u>squash</u>, to cite but one example, originally had nothing to do with (as we now know it) a vegetable, an athletic contest, or a violent act.

In fact the word can be traced back to early hieroglyphic tablets, from which the pictorial symbol for <u>squ</u> translated loosely as "the smell of burning," while the more familiar symbol for <u>ash</u> is known to have signified "goat cheese." Thusly, the combined word <u>squ-ash</u>, in its original Nilotic form and intent, meant "the smell of burning goat cheese." (Annual festivals centered on the curd of the goat, and involved sacrificing a portion of the yellowish sponge to Ra-Curdl, the god of cheese. When sizzled over open fires, the silky goo often became an unintentional "burnt offering").

There are thousands of such examples, of course, even a superficial treatment of which fills literal volumes in itself. Indeed, the ongoing word-game represents for many a kind of linguistic treasure hunt which never seems to lose its scholarly seduction, with each new and exhilarating discovery merely fueling the intellectual flames of the already-smitten.

One classic example is the term "barbed wire," which in its original context was neither "barbed" nor "wire" as we know and use the terms today.

Deriving its catchy name from its French co-inventors, Pierre D'Barbed (dee-bar-bed) and Jean-Claude Wire (weere), the prototype material was an inexpensive but extremely durable early acrylic used extensively throughout the south of France and the adjacent Pyrenees following its initial appearance there in the mid-1720s.

Although its original utilitarian purpose was indeed to assure the confinement of French livestock within the meadows and fields of their respective owners, the early acrylic eventually proved a disconcertingly impractical solution to the age-old problem of keeping one's animals separate from those of his neighbors. Nor was the discovery of the notorious impracticality without a certain irony.

The livestock, it seems - and more particularly the sheep - apparently liked the feel of the smooth acrylic against their sides, an attraction that kept them close to fence-lines for long periods of time. Not only did this result in peripheral over-grazing that eventually became a genuinely serious problem in itself; it also was to prove a classic example of "invention arising from idleness," as Agatha Christie would describe it more than two centuries later.

As it happened, the fleecy creatures soon learned that by judicious plucking of the plastic material strung from post to post, they could produce a primitive, although quite stirring rendition of *La Marseillaise*, a discovery that caused no little vexation among the concerned populace as all patriotic Frenchmen within earshot suddenly found themselves leaping to absolutely appropriate attention at embarrassingly and decidedly inappropriate moments.

As one might imagine, this quickly became a nuisance - so much so, in fact, that by summer's end of the year 1731, the venerable Livestock Alliance of Southern France voted to a man to give the incommodious matter its highest priority. Nor, as one might reasonably expect from the demented minds of elected officials, did this prove merely another example of placating lip-service.

Many of the LASF officials were themselves residents of the areas in question, and had on more than one occasion been subjected to the annoyance of the ovine-initiated national anthem inundating the countryside at predictably awkward moments during the long days and even longer nights. (One farmer-legislator described an outhouse experience that flushed the cheeks of several in attendance; yet a second related the interruption of an even more delicate matter, drawing mini-titters of self-conscious laughter from the assemblage).

In short, the problem being personal as well as constituental, they meant business.

Trial and error, those mischievous twins of progress, eventually brought the frustrated Frenchmen to the threshold of discovery. To their delight, they experimentally determined that, unlike the smooth and clearly pleasurable acrylic, the abrasiveness of rusted metal strips was decidedly not to the liking of the various beasts, particularly when spliced at ominous intervals with sharp and nasty steel points. By 1739, the new product was tested and found true.

By that time, the trade name D'Barbed-Wire had become something of a generic term for virtually anything strung between two posts (occasional sausage links included). It carried over quite naturally to the newly-perfected metal substitute, and barbed wire, as we know the product today, turned out to be the solution to a dilemma that had witnessed thousands of agitated French farmers painfully torn between practicality and patriotism. With the eventual mass advent of the new material, the dozen-year nightmare of sudden and unexpected musical concerts was brought to an abrupt end, albeit one meadow at a time.

The name thereafter passed intact into English, of course, and is used to this day in such diverse locales as Bangor, Bozeman, and Buenos Aires - this despite the probability that not one native out of a thousand anywhere is remotely cognizant of the agricultural heritage passed on to him by a couple of innovative and unassuming French lads name Pierre D'Barbed and Jean-Claude Wire, truly the unknown soldiers of modern fencing.

Their industry-wide reputation of the "Fathers of Fencing" has been brought into serious question only once, when it was discovered that the Mayans, who are claimed to have existed somewhat earlier than the Frenchmen (or, for that matter, than France itself), did make use of a thatched metal product they called chane-linque.

It, however, was not utilized at all in a fashion that would challenge barbed wire as the world's first-known device dedicated exclusively to enclosure. In fact, the Mayans used chane-linque in the manufacture of a delicacy they called Quixocuxul, consisting of enormously thick 10-foot sections of pasta forcibly rammed through thatched metal openings onto gigantic baking sheets. It is said that an entire Mayan village could subsist on a single one of these basted and baked pasta pylons for up to six months, using the hardened stump-splits thereafter to hold up lean-to shacks, aging smokehouses, mini-aqueducts and the sundry aged and infirm among the scattered New World Indian villages.

# BETWEEN EACH BUN SOME RAIN MUST FALL

C: 2011 – Dr. Ron Pataky ---- Custom-Ransom-Notes.com

Although the news is coming as a terrific jolt to delicatessen owners and aficionados from Bangor to Petaluma, the facts are quite incontrovertible: the well-known phrase lox and bagels was never intended to represent either (a) something Jewish, or (b) an ethnic euphemism describing fish on a bun. Its derivation, in fact, is Scottish --- in its original, uncorrupted form lochs and beagles.

Loch, of course, is the Scottish word for lake. Beagle is the Scottish word for beagle.

The term first came into popular usage during the frequent Scottish monster hunts of the late 1770s (long before lox and bagels), during which period the ever-intrepid Scots gamely rode their hounds (beagles) to the lakes (lochs) at the slightest hint of yet another reported monster sighting, an occurrence that took place on an average of twice weekly between 1771 and the present century.

For more than 200 years, the Scots, a closed-mouth people by nature, revealed little to outsiders concerning their local sport, preferring instead to await that day when an actual monster might be netted (or, a century-plus later, at least detained long enough to be properly photographed).

This behavior, of course, comes as no surprise to anthropologists, who have long been aware that nearly all societies are keenly sensitive concerning their local legends. The sturdy Scots were just that, preferring caution to the possibility of being victimized by a hoax that would bring the derision of strangers pouring down on them like a rare Highland monsoon. (They seem deliciously fond, by the way, of mentioning Piltdown man and the Hitler diaries to those mocking their cautious ways).

How, in about 1779, the phrase made the intriguing transition from a Scottish dragon hunt to a Jewish delicacy remains a mystery to even the most steadfast etymologists, although such mutations are not nearly as rare as one might think (our recent revelation concerning the true origins of swish cheese come to mind).

Whatever the case, the story of how the facts finally emerged, leapfrogging the Atlantic into the dazzling neon milieu of American deli aficionados, is a brief but utterly fascinating yarn in itself.

Involved was a young, moderately successful sports buff named MacGregor Woods who, having saved several years for the vacation of his dreams, finally was able to make the trip from his Brooklyn home to the north of Scotland, where he planned to fulfill a lifelong ambition to play the world-famous St. Andrews golf course.

His first evening there found him giddily ensconced in a local gin mill, scarcely able to contain the excitement of his scheduled tee-off time early the following morning. On being approached by the waiter, Woods didn't even bother to consult the menu. "I think I'd like some lox and bagels," he fairly bubbled at the aproned figure. (Being from Brooklyn, he naturally had doted on the zesty salmon delight since his immediate post-Farina days).

Completely caught up in anticipation of the coming dawn at St. Andrews, Woods was oblivious to the rather queer expression that briefly crossed the waiter's face; or, for that matter, to the decidedly unorthodox way the waiter muttered to himself while brusquely snatching the menu from Woods' hands and stalking away.

It was about thirty minutes later when, to Woods' utter astonishment, an elderly Scottish gentleman approached the corner table at which Woods dreamily sat, leading, of all things, a clearly enthusiastic beagle hound (which promptly lifted his leg to mark the occasion). "Ah'm here about your lochs and beagles, laddie," the old fellow began. "Here's your map an' light. Your horse is tethered out front as we speak and knows well the way."

Woods, of course, was flabbergasted; and indeed, it was several hours before the intricacies of the misunderstanding were unraveled to the satisfaction of all, after which, to the unanimous delight of those privy, both hearty laughter and good Scotch whisky abounded into the night.

Less than a week later, having fulfilled his lifelong dream of playing St. Andrews, Woods found himself back home in Brooklyn, where he immediately began regaling the chaps at one corner deli after another with the hilarious details of his memorable experience. The story quickly spread throughout Brooklyn and Queens, moving thereafter into Manhattan and westward. At last report it had reached Decatur, Illinois, where a Pakistani deli owner learned of it via a long-distance call from his brother-in-law in southeast Cincinnati.

No story concerning lochs and beagles, of course, would be complete without at least nominal mention of the legendary Loch Ness monster, reputedly the grand-daddy of them all.

Despite literally hundreds of rumored sightings through the years, the reputation "Nessy" holds as grand dragon of all local behemoths is open to serious question. Indeed, most photographs of the elusive beast are considered by experts to be either the result of freak atmospheric conditions, or simply out-and-out fakes. The bottom line is that there exists not a single shred of substantive evidence that the big fellow exists at all (or, for that matter, ever did).

A much smaller monster, however, allegedly bagged in 1917 and affectionately baptized "Angus" by the enthusiastic gentry of the time, is said to have lived nearly two-dozen years in congenial captivity before finally expiring in 1940, one of the many victims of that year's dreadful epidemic of hoof and scale disease.

Angus (or at least the cured business claimed to have been Angus) has since been stuffed, and presently (as of 2011) adorns the huge entrance hall of Prince Charles' Firth of Clyde country manor, scarcely 15 kilometers from the shallow lagoon where he allegedly washed up more than 90 years ago.

Tourists are able to grab a peek at the somewhat frayed and pocked remains for a nominal fee, and the curious demand for "original Angus teeth" continues to keep area kilns fired up around the clock. (For the ladies, Angus bonnets and gloves are a favorite, keeping local tanners busy as well).

Ironically, no one seems in the least put-off by the known fact (indeed publicly advertised!) that sales of "original" Angus teeth had, by 1995, exceeded 17 million in number. Even the most cursory calculation, after all, would be thought enough to alert all but the dullest traveler to the probability that such a number exceeds by a considerable amount the total number of, say, shark teeth on the entire planet, be the sharks living or dead, large or small, fossilized or stuffed.

But it seems to matter not. The response of one dowdy

society-type from Palm Springs, California, while perhaps not altogether typical, nevertheless seems an accurate reflection of normal "collector" attitudes.

"Who cares," she sniffed contemptuously. "When I finally completed my mule-egg collection a few years back, I got terribly, terribly depressed, nearly losing my very will to carry on. Now, oh joy unspeakable, I have something new to live for."

No one uttered a word of rebuttal. And certainly no Scot.

# FREUDIAN SLIPS (AND OTHER UNDERGARMENTS)

**Dr. Nicolai Gustav Clook**

Flagrant misapplication of the utterly ambiguous term "Freudian Slip" has given rise to the near-fanatical belief during the past century or so that the phrase has something to do with "psychoanalysis," a popular Austrian parlor game cynically referred to in select caustic circles as "Viennese Roulette."

In actuality, the term seems more likely an archeological one, apparently having more than a little something to do with an obscure Native American people called the *Freudian Indians,* who lived along the banks of the Squash River in southern Illinois, near present-day Carbondale, from roughly 200-900 A. D.

Recent excavations of burial sites and small prehistoric tree-villages tell us the Freudians were a relatively tall, big-boned race of sedentary tree-dwellers who were significantly advanced for their time, both with regard to tool-making and wardrobe. In addition to being the first recorded native entrepreneurs to have *labeled* their goods (many pottery samples are stamped "Freudian made"), they also were, as far as we know, the first society anywhere in which at least the more affluent females routinely wore undergarments.

This mild curiosity probably would have remained a mere footnote to history were it not for the fact of the term "Freudian Slip" somehow having carried over into modern usage as a vague remnant of an otherwise obscure, albeit advanced, society. Ironically, since one almost never hears the terms today, both the Freudian Bra *and* Freudian Panties predated the evolution of the Freudian Slip by several hundred years – and were, not surprisingly, infinitely more crucial within the extremely complex social structure of the Freudians.

(As an interesting aside, several recently discovered Freudian undergarments apparently were of an early designer variety, featuring the red ochre outline of a small fawn and the logo, *Running Bubble,* stenciled on the left front hems.

Unearthed in the same series of Illinois digs, incidentally, were shreds of the short-lived Freudian Corset, which seems to have been worn exclusively by males, and then only for ceremonial purposes. Best evidence, however, is that this apparent social aberration lasted only briefly. Indeed, of the entire 700-year existence of the Freudians, the so-called "Corset Period" seems to have begun and ended abruptly during the apparently unbearably sweltering summer of 423 A. D.

Whatever significance this newest information may or may not have is perhaps best left to future historians, although present-day confusion surrounding the Illinois Freudians and their curious link to both Austria and psychoanalysis is frustrating, to say the very, very least.

One theory holds that an ancient splinter group of the original Freudians somehow made their way to Austria (they were, of course, expert canoeists), there to exist in near-total isolation for perhaps a thousand years, only to surface in the mid-1800s as a tightly-knit coterie of eccentric designers of dainties who, according to one source, spoke the local dialect with a conspicuous Illinois accent.

Still another theory is that a Viennese therapist named Von Poopsie somehow became aware of these prehistoric frilleries and grew obsessed with a possible connection between their undeniable allure and the sudden spate of bedwetting that characterized the decade from 1843-53 in eastern Austria.

(Von Poopsie, trivialists may recall, is the doctor who gained a modicum of notoriety on documenting the first recorded incidence of a man experiencing schizophrenia and déjà vu at the same time, a curious phenomenon that resulted in only *half* of him sensing he had encountered the same situation before. The other half bitterly complained that *he'd* been in Innsbruck, agonizing through a root canal at the time).

Yet a third possibility, although discounted by most as too far-fetched even to contemplate, is that the term is completely unrelated to the Illinois Freudians, but evolved instead from the copious meanderings of a local quack named Siegfried Freudian, who put forth the dotty notion that our nightly dreams – are you ready for this? – are inextricably interwoven with virtually every abnormality known to humankind, from scabies and gout to lumbago, PMS, and the vapors. The fact that Dr. Freudian smoked twenty cigars a day and was hopelessly hooked on cocaine perhaps partially explained this curious conclusion.

Whatever the eventual case, one puzzling aspect of Illinois Freudian culture seems likely to remain unsolved.

Southern Illinois is, along with New Jersey, arguably among the bleakest, most God-forsaken areas on the planet, which naturally causes one to wonder what a society as obviously advanced as the Freudians was doing there in the first place. The Ozark region, for instance, a mere five-day paddle to the west, was and is infinitely more scenic, not to mention being an area of cheaper energy sources, lower taxes, and a more acceptable year-round pollen count.

For all of their garment and tool-making technology, it remains a curiosity that the Freudians were unaware of this, although it does dramatically illustrate the festering information void that eventually would give rise to television in general, and National Geographic specials in particular. Electricity, of course, was still some years away in the 600s.

It is ironic, by the way, that primary among the sponsors of these self-same National Geographic specials are manufacturers of the very undies the Freudians so adroitly spawned a thousand or more years ago – not even to mention the tired flotilla of designer garments being passed off as innovative to an unsuspecting public. Observed one social commentator of the situation: "I'll bet the Freudians are simply fuming … and probably turning over in what's left of their tattered Tupperware!"

Which brings us to the final fact to come forth from our study of the Freudians and their centuries-shredded undergarments. Twentieth-century scientists now concur with eco-junkies of this modern era: yes, it now is a proven fact that plastic (in all of its manifestations) does indeed require a thousand or more years to properly "return to nature." If you have the time, go ahead and wait. If not, you might consider recycling.

# WW II AND THE GOLDEN DENTURES

## History at a Glance

C: 2011 – Dr. Ron Pataky Custom-Ransom-Notes.com

New light has been thrown on a legendary remark attributed to World War II General of the Army Douglas MacArthur by documents recently discovered in the vaults of the venerable Guttenberg Archives.

According to the documents, which include an apparently long-forgotten interview granted by the general to a little-known and equally obscure news reporter in September of 1946, the celebrated MacArthur quote "I shall return" was never a promise at all, as history most certainly has suggested, but rather, according to the general himself, "an out and out threat."

This startling and sordid revelation, with due respect to the courageous Filipino people, apparently was lost to history for nearly six decades as the result of a monumental misunderstanding that became, as it were, self-perpetuating.

It seems the original five-page written interview, on being mailed to the reporter's wire service back in the states, had been slugged "RETURN," a perfectly logical choice, of course, in light of its subject matter.

The unfortunate effect, however, was sadly misinterpreted, construed instead as if the package had been stamped "RETURN TO SENDER," result of which was that the interview spent the next 32 years in the capable hands of the U. S. Post Office, where it was efficiently "returned" back and forth repeatedly between its original source and its original destination.

How it eventually fell into the hands of the Gutenberg Archives perhaps 20 years ago remains a mystery, although the Post Office did initiate an investigation into the matter in April of 1976. The investigation was sidetracked for more than nine years, however, when the original inquiry was inadvertently mailed without a stamp.

In any event, the interview finally has resurfaced; and despite the intrigue surrounding its recent discovery, several history-changing facts are now known.

As witnessed by Filipino attorney named Llamapampas, among others (and as confirmed at one time by the general himself), the threat originally was directed by MacArthur towards a Manila dentist named Vagabundo. Gist of the spat (which only incidentally was to affect the outcome of the entire Pacific war) was the smoldering accusation that Dr. Vagabundo had stubbornly withheld a magnificent set of custom gold dentures at a time when they were desperately needed by the general, claiming a balance due of $4.18.

When the gold dentures had not been delivered as promised by the fall of Corregidor, the general, never a patient man, became virtually apoplectic, brandishing his baton at Dr. Vagabundo in a manner perceived by a number of witnesses as menacing and literally bellowing the since-famous "I shall return." (The dentist's receptionist, it is reported, was treated on the spot for an instantaneous and severe attack of hives; two patients in the waiting room also suffered shortness of breath).

As it happened, Dr. Vagabundo's dental drill was

inadvertently wired into the same frequency as Radio Manila, and the threat was heard in what seemed to be unmistakable terms throughout the whole of the Philippines and Southeast Asia, being, as history has long since recorded, incorrectly interpreted as a promise.

Events of the next few years were nothing short of incredible. Following the earlier attack on Pearl Harbor, of course, the American fleet was painstakingly rebuilt, eventually culminating in the Battle of the Coral Sea (1942), in which the Americans checked the southward expansion of the Japanese once and for all. The island war swung into full force, with the Americans inching their tortuous way toward the full victory that eventually would be theirs. Slowly, island by bloody island, the U. S. Navy and Marines fought their way back in the general direction of the Philippines.

A major boost to the heroic American thrust occurred when the Japanese, to the astonishment of virtually everyone, decided not to invade Australia. It was to be a much-regretted decision, based as it happens on one of the few genuinely humorous episodes of the long and tragic war.

It seems the Japanese high command in early 1942 received what was thought to be a secret memo directly from the emperor, the would-be communiqué cleverly disguised as a captured Chinese menu. To their reluctant amazement, they quickly discovered that "won ton," when spelled backward, becomes "not now." Thinking that they had indeed decoded an order from the emperor himself, they immediately cancelled plans to attack the Australian mainland, turning their attention instead to the southeast and Malaysia. In many ways, this served to clear the path for the Americans, with whom they would have clashed in perhaps the biggest battle of the war had they continued their drive southward to Australia.

Eventually, of course, MacArthur did return to the Philippines, thereby fulfilling his threat. By this time, however, Dr. Vagabundo, a reputed Jesuit groupie as far back as the early 1930s, had forsaken his dental practice to take actual Jesuit vows, and had journeyed to the island of Mindanao, where he worked among the lame and destitute until his death in 1987.

The gold dentures were used for a brief time as a doorstop by a Japanese air force colonel named Hadiki Hakimoto, later to be shamed by the incommodious nickname "The Chicken Colonel" as the result of his having flown 147 kamikaze missions without so much as denting his fuselage. Hakimoto, for whom "safety first" had always been paramount, was employed after the war as plant safety manager for the Sony Corporation's Hokkaido Division. He retired in 1974, and spent his remaining golden years breeding rare miniature nasturtiums, which he shipped to ardent collectors throughout the world. His colorful "Rising Sun" hybrid remains a favorite everywhere, and has taken first prize in countless nasturtium festivals, including the esteemed Sudanese Floral Expo.

The infamous dentures have long since disappeared; and to his death, Hakimoto resolutely continued to disavow any knowledge whatsoever of their mysterious whereabouts. Their fascinating story, however, is presently a major motion picture, brought to you by the gifted people who gave us Raiders of the Lost Ark. It is scheduled for release in the year 2015, and is tentatively titled Robbers of the Golden Dentures.

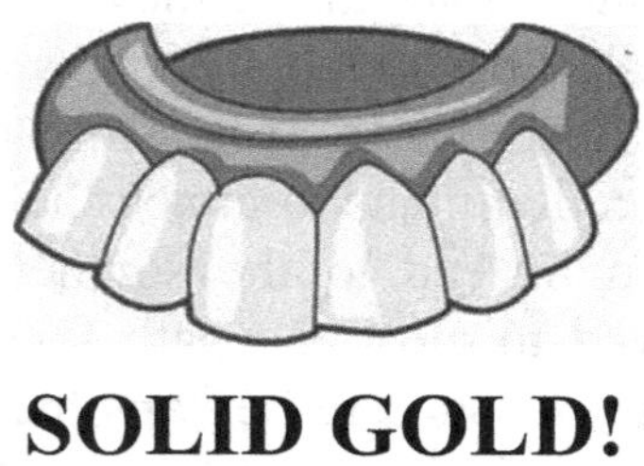

**SOLID GOLD!**

# THE NEARLY UNBELIEVABLE ORDEAL OF PVT. HALEY SCROGGS


Custom-Ransom-Notes.com

**August 12, 2010** -- A Confederate Army private who for the past 149 years had been under the impression that the War Between the States continued to rage has been found living in a deep-woods cave in the remote Yew Mountain region south of Bergoo, West Virginia.

Haley Scroggs, who was discovered late this past summer by a group of Bergoo milkmaids on a berry outing, says he was a mere lad of 15 or so when, in the fall of 1861, he left his father's small tobacco spread near Toad Landing, Tennessee, to join the ranks of the legendary First Tennessee Volunteers. All he had with him, he says, was "some grease, some jerky, a long rifle, and whatever clothes I almost had on."

Scroggs, who estimates his age at "a hundred an' some," says he eventually lost track of the years completely when the giant oak he had faithfully notched to mark the passing days "finally took one notch too many an' keeled right over." That was, he says, "maybe eighty-ninety years ago." Depending on the month of his birth (which he has long since forgotten), Scroggs today would be about 162 years old, making him, so far as is known, the oldest living American Civil War veteran.

The Tennessean claims he had seen battle in half a dozen or more bloody skirmishes prior to the morning some months after joining the volunteers when he was kicked in the head by a regimental mule. Thereafter, except for periodic flashes of lucidity, he has been unable to recall events and their sequence with any clarity at all.

"I know I was in a tent somewheres," he recalled last week to an interviewer in Roanoke, where he'd been taken for cleaning. "Jist a few days, though, as I recollect. Then they sent me packin'. Said I might git a mite dizzy now an' again, but I should head back an' find my outfit."

From that day until his discovery last month, Scroggs claims to have seen but one other human being in the nearly 149 years he spent in hiding, foraging for his daily sustenance, living primarily on berries, nuts, and an occasional kill, ever on the lookout for "blue-coated busybodies." His single human visitor, an itinerant preacher who "might'a been saved but shore was lost," happened by less than a year after Scroggs had stumbled onto the cave entrance of what was to become his permanent home.

"He was a powerful help," Scroggs recalls with obvious sarcasm. "Asked him if'n he knew the way to Pikeston. He hawed on for near an hour, and then said: 'Son, if I'd been headin' for there, I shore wouldn't a started from here.' Yep, he was a great help...regular Dan'l Boone. Last I saw of him, he was headed off in about three directions. Good riddance, I said."

And Haley's recollections of daily life after that? "Well, it comes an' goes, don't ya know." Of one thing, however, he is certain: For the next 140-plus years or so, Private Haley Scroggs, still under the impression that he served the cause of the Confederacy, did not see or speak with another human.

Scroggs, who seems amazingly spry for a man of his advanced years, also is clearly gifted with a lively sense of humor. Indeed, it may have been this obvious blessing that kept him going during the century-plus of sweltering summers and fierce winters in the wild. Describing these incredible years (during which he seldom ventured more than 100 yards from his brush-hidden cave, and then only to occasionally ravage a wild onion patch nearby), he stated without hesitation that his two worst enemies were loneliness and boredom.

"The nights was the worst," he recalls. "Specially durin' the first few years. Strange noises durin' the night. Black as Satan's lair. Made a man skittish for sure. Come mornin' those early years I'd be as jumpy as a long-tailed cat in a roomful a rockin' chairs." Asked if he'd occasionally gotten homesick for Toad Landing, he stared for a moment at the distant hills. "Does a one-legged monkey walk with a bounce?" he countered quietly.

Since young Haley had been the only son born to Cody and Clarissa Scroggs, it is not surprising that no trace of the family name can be found today in or around Toad Landing. He did have nine sisters, however, and it was suggested by one reporter that Scroggs might have some kin back home if any of his sisters had married.

"Not likely," he responded, shaking his head doubtfully and chuckling. "Them gals was ugly...powerful ugly." He thought for a moment. "Reckon Urla Sue were prob'ly the pick of the litter," he recalled with a perceptible shudder, "an' <u>she</u> had a face that would'a stopped a paddle wheel.

“Whooshy,” he exhaled (using his favorite expression). He

giggled aloud at the memory, dribbling a green substance from his leathery lips in the process. Noticing the interviewer's startled response to the greenish liquid, Scroggs explained that he had searched unsuccessfully for wild tobacco for a year or more, only to finally settle on drying and chewing the area's abundant apple mint. "Puffed a bit, too," he added. "Helped pass the time."

Scroggs seemed mildly pleased to learn that the war had actually been over for some time, and apparently was not at all surprised to hear that the Northern army had achieved its eventual success. "Never thought we'd win anyway," he said somewhat contemptuously. "Not with fellas like that Captain Jipson or Jepson or whatever his name was runnin' things. Never did think that fella's clothesline was connected at both ends. That man had two speeds...dead in his tracks an' backwards."

(Learning from a local historian that the captain in question, A. W. Jepston, Jr., of Culpepper County, Virginia, had died of endemic warts during the dreadful plague of 1887, Scroggs reflected for a moment, then nailed a dragonfly in mid-flight with an awesomely-aimed jet of green chaw. "Don't reckon I'll miss 'im much," he concluded).

Among the many extraordinary things about Scroggs is his unfailing optimism, which any number of younger men found delightfully refreshing during the interview. Example: Asked what he plans to do now that he is, so to speak, out of the cave, he stunned the young reporters by announcing his intention (with some sense of urgency, it was noted), to "find me a good woman."

And who knows? Among the many gifts and honors heaped upon the grizzled veteran by various companies and civic groups was a supposedly humorous "lifetime membership" in the Norfolk chapter of an outfit called Matchmakers International. Incredibly enough, a newspaper account of the presentation already has drawn what seems to be a sincere interest from a 19-year-old Sassarillo

County lass who explains: "Most of my girlfriends seem to be looking for a father-figure. Me, I've always been more interested in an ancestor type."

Scroggs, of course, was elated (and palpably confident) on hearing of the young woman's apparently sincere inquiry. Sensing skepticism as he scanned the faces of the young reporters, he made a stab at setting the record straight. "Don't let these ol' bones fool you," he chortled, proudly stroking his magnificent black furry parka. "I didn't git this bear skin at no general store."

# On the Sublime Raptures Of Interruptions

C: 2011 – Dr. Ron Pataky ---- Custom-Ransom-Notes.com

Barney Brantickle, the popular tire re-capper and highly regarded Chihuahua breeder from Dalrymple, Mississippi, spends hundreds of hours monthly on what many consider a pair of highly unusual hobbies. The first involves collecting video "interruptions," while the second is concentrated on capturing and preserving the very essence of bubbles -- bubbles that would otherwise have popped in a matter of atmospheric seconds. While we're primarily concerned today with the subject of "interruptions," the Brantickle bubble hobby certainly worth a brief mention here.

Brantickle, who works side by side with his wife Bertie, says he first became interested in bubbles, "One afternoon when the kids were blowing the things, and I saw just how beautiful and fragile they were. I just naturally wondered if I could find a way to keep them."

What he and Bertie did that evening was to purchase their own bubble-blowing pipe. Within a few hours ("certainly before midnight," he says), the couple had discovered that they could actually preserve the fruit of their bubble-pipe labors if they managed to "hit them real, real quick" with Bertie's "Neutron" hairspray. "We would blow and blow until we got a really big bubble," he says, "then the one of us not blowing at the time would run around the thing and spray like holy heck. Eventually, it worked!"

Barney and Bertie offer "Bubble Evenings" several times a year, at which time they dazzle small groups of friends and neighbors with the hundreds of hardened bubbles they've managed to capture and retain through the years -- softball-sized and hard as coreless granite, the jewel-like spheres refract available light in truly stunning fashion from atop various pedestals placed like a mini hazard course throughout the room. As one bowled-over observer observed last week, "They're something to see, all right."

A Brantickle niece, Sookie Mae, also is "bubble-active," according to Bertie. She recently graduated from Dalrymple High School, and plans to study journalism at the university in the fall. The Brantickles are justifiably proud of their Sookie Mae, who recently had her first rhyme published in the popular Bubble Quarterly. It read:

**A hole in a bubble**
**Presumes bubble trouble**
**(The role of a hole's to diminish!)**
**But short of a hole**
**As grim is the role**
**Of a scratch in the bubble's clear finish!**

(NOTE: The published poem did receive a modicum of critical response, mostly from bubble enthusiasts who felt it was excessively jocular and degraded bubbles to the level of, as one sourpuss writer described it, "second-class inanimates."). While the bubble-hobby continues to be a community delight in and around Dalrymple, it is the "interruption" business that has grabbed the attention and interest of the press, not only throughout Mississippi, but through the entire American southeast as well. Indeed, the Brantickle name has become known far and wide in recent years.

The "interruptions" are carefully videotaped occurrences of the universally-familiar logo, "Stand by … we are experiencing technical difficulties" from television stations across the country.

Brantickle estimates that he and his wife have taped close to five thousand hours of multifarious versions since beginning their impressive collection nearly eight years ago. "They drive most people crazy," he said during a recent interview on Channel 47's popular weekly show, Mississippi Hobbyist. "But me 'n Bertie just love the doggoned things. Honestly, you would not believe the difference from one region to another! They're just … well, beautiful, once a body starts paying attention."

Barney and Bertie grew up "dirt poor," about forty miles apart, he in Gulfport, where his daddy worked at Gulfport's leading sandwich and bait shop, and Bertie down the road in Picayune, where her folks, running a ramshackle business known as the Harkness Insectery, raised lightning bugs and worms, the former for research at Tulane University, and the worms as commercial bait.

Among Harkness customers was Bubba's Sandwich & Bait Emporium down in Gulfport, and Barney and Bertie would finally meet at the annual Bait Society Dance. They were married eight short weeks later – still, as they relate it, "poor as homeless kittens." Early on in their blissful union, Bertie wrote home to her mother and daddy that:

**We have a roof**
**Over our head**
**Who could ask for more?**
**And soon as we**
**Can afford a bed**
**We're gonna get a floor**

Mother Harkness (Bertie's maiden name) thought the ditty so cute that she passed it on to the Picayune Clarion, where it ran on page one the following day under the title of "Newlyweds."

Barney and Bertie have taped most of their collection themselves, making frequent trips to nearby states, where, "we hole up in a bargain motel with our camera and three TV sets, and wait for one sort of calamity or another to happen." (They've affectionately dubbed their ever-present video camera, "Calamity Jane," with a back-up unit referred to simply as "CJ-2.").

Barney views their hobby as anything but repetitious, comparing it to the efforts of "those fellows who're always running around photographing tornados." Says Brantickle, "Heck, it's easy to say once you've seen one tornado, you've seen them all. Anyone who knows their stuff knows that's just bugwash. Same thing with 'interruptions' (as they are referred to by serious hobbyists). It's just a matter of being at the right place at the right time – tornados or interruptions. The minute me and Bertie see a set begin to spit and wobble, well sir, we get that camera cranking right now, believe you me!"

Although the Brantickles estimate their collection as being about ninety per cent the result of their own taping efforts, they do trade tapes with five or six other collectors, including one in American Samoa and another in Ecuador. Among their most treasured is an "interruption" of an actual assassination attempt in the latter country. "This guy comes running up to some local Ecuadorian bigwig, shouting fatal intentions and waving a gigantic machete, and 'bleep,' suddenly – in Spanish, of course – there's our old friend, 'Stand by, we are experiencing technical difficulties,' right there on the screen, big as life, so to speak." Thanks to a trade with their Ecuadorian friend, the Brantickles are the proud owners of their very own videotape of the almost-incident. "It's quite a collector's item," he acknowledges with obvious delight.

At Bertie's urging, Barney mentions another favorite – the only known copy of an "interruption" that took place during the final days of a now-defunct Hattiesburg independent then known as WHEW-TV, which (coincidentally?) turns out to have been the nation's last steam-driven television broadcasting station. "

Believe it or not, the thing is nearly two hours long," says Bertie, "Guess they had quite a blow-out that day." Adds Barney with obvious pride, "I reckon it might be worth ten, maybe twelve dollars to a collector. One guy on Guadalcanal IS interested … but the dude wants to haggle a bit. He needs to remember that I'm the only game in town, so to speak."

The Branticklеs first became interested in their hobby as the result of sheer happenstance. "We was down in Biloxi," explains Barney. "That was in October, 1996, remember, Bertie? We was there for the annual Guild Coast Tire Re-cappers Convention. "It was, oh, maybe an hour or so before we was to leave for the turtle roast – remember, Bertie, you and me was watching the Andy Griffith Show. Anyways, that set started flickering and spitting so hard it almost jumped off the table. Being new to the game, of course, we weren't sure what the heck was happening." "Maybe two, three minutes later, the interruption flashed on the screen. Pretty as anything you've ever seen … bright orange, flickering on and off and saying, you know, 'Stand by … we are experiencing technical difficulties.'

I said to Bertie, 'Wow, that'd make a pretty picture.' She said, 'Why don't you run out to the truck and get the Kodak.' We only had our still camera then. So I did just that. "Well sir, I'll tell you … when we got them pictures back from Pearl-Mart and saw how beautiful they turned out … well, I guess you could say the rest is history."

The Brantickles bought their first video camera about three months later, and have not ("far as we know") missed taping a single interruption in the area since. "We keep three TV sets going all the time as a rule," Barney explains enthusiastically. "The camera's on a revolving tripod. The second we see a possible interruption in the making ("You learn the signs to look for," he confides with a wink), well sir, we just spin that sucker around don't ya know, and we're ready for business!"

Interruptions of just about any dramatic moment are the most desirable, says Brantickle, citing the final moments of a murder mystery or a sudden-death field goal as classic examples. "Course, interrupting a presidential speech or a tornado warning wouldn't be too shabby, either," he grins. And what might be the most collectable hypothetical interruption of them all?

Hard to say," Barney reflects, glancing over at the equally contemplative Bertie. "Tell you one I'd give the pick of the litter for, though … hearing a broadcaster say something like, 'We interrupt this program to bring you the following urgent announcement from the White House,' followed by a burp and a shudder, and then, 'Stand by … we are experiencing technical difficulties.'" He looks over at Bertie, her eyes glazed over with excitement. "Yep, that'd be one for the "bug box" all right."

Unabashedly, the Brantickles' fondest dream is to eventually interest a television producer in a project that would find their 5,000-plus hours of interruptions edited down to "say, ten hours, maybe … you know, for a five-part mini-series or something like that on one of the networks. "I tell you, that Johnny Carson would've been the one to narrate the thing," he says dreamily. ("Wasn't he a stitch," Bertie adds with a giggle. "And so cute, too, God rest his soul!").

Barney reflects for a moment, "Wonder if any of his programs was ever hit with an interruption…" His voice trails off. Their bubble pipe and a can of Bertie's Neutron untouched on a nearby shelf, Barney and Bertie continue to stare at the three sets in their darkened dining room. Waiting.

# LETHARGY: AN ODE TO SQUALOR

C: 2011 – Dr. Ron Pataky ---- Custom-Ransom-Notes.com

**Psssst .... filthy picture ceramics!**

The first notoriety of its bleak 176-year history recently came to Lethargy, Oklahoma, a small, wretched huddle of humanity in the westernmost plains portion of the Sooner State's forlorn panhandle; and it was, in the dreary vernacular of the area's squalid citizenry, "a double-doozy."

According to a recent disclosure by the Department of the Interior, Lethargy is the only city in the world of more than 4,000 inhabitants to boast of no accomplishments whatsoever. Ironically, this dismal distinction has earned the sodden slum a questionable place in the *Guinness Book of World Records.*

Incredibly enough, Lethargy does not even appear on most maps of Oklahoma, a curiosity that has been described by some state officials, whose dealings with the city's inert population have been something less than ideal through the years, as "the definitive anonymity."

The history of the place is as uninspiring as its present woeful condition. It was founded in 1836 by an indolent gaggle of "pioneers," who, having been expelled from a wagon train because of their insufferable personal habits, decided in typically languid fashion that they were "bored with travel anyway." As thunderheads auger rain, so Lethargy's first citizens proved a jolting harbinger of its insipid future, and the mudhole was off to a beginning that was inauspicious in the extreme.

Indeed, its sole attractions to this day are water (delivered with routine frequency via funnel cloud), and a uniquely blended soil composition that fluctuates, depending on the time and exact location of the most recent twister, between a gritty, utterly oppressive silt, and an inextricable muck next to which quicksand is positively appealing. Observed one motorist whose lot it was to stall there last summer, "It is not a pretty picture."

A recent independent study conducted by the Federal Emergency Management folks reveals for the first time several pertinent facts.

Lethargy does not have, nor has it ever had, a police force ("Course, ain't nuthin' to steal so we don't have no crime neither," remarked one revolting specimen). Nor does it have a fire department, although this, too, seems of little consequence to the apathetic townsfolk. Their point: since there is no wood in the region, everything is made of mud. Since everything is made of mud, there is nothing that will, under any circumstances, combust.

Stranger still is the fact that Lethargy has no city officials. In its only election ever, rather hastily mounted in 1943, the outcome proved predictably innocuous when no one bothered to run for any of the city's several tentative offices. Asked how they manage to run things from day to day, a second disgusting citizen spat down a trouser leg and drawled, "We git by."

The city has no telephones, and but a single television set. The latter sits on some magazines behind the cracked and yellowed glass window of Hubble's Hardware, where a handful of folks convene daily between four and five in the afternoon to watch re-re-runs of "Red Ryder" and "Sky King." There is but a single barber in the entire area; and though he cuts hair free, he does charge a small admission fee to watch.

The fact is that Lethargy seems in a constant state of virtual siesta. People think absolutely nothing of falling into a deep sleep wherever and whenever the mood strikes them, and even more personal habits frequently are not given the discretion common decency would normally dictate.

Nor (need we add?) is Lethargy the quintessential moral community, particularly where per capita alcohol consumption is concerned. The quoted remark of yet another local lout is typical. "Good thing we don't have no po-lice," he slobbered, "or they'd be arrestin' folks for *sober* drivin'!" It is a remark that veritably epitomizes the prevailing attitude in Lethargy, where anything foul and disgusting can and does elicit spasms of cackling laughter at every turn.

There are no churches of any denomination. To extend one's education beyond grade three (which can only be accomplished two counties away in any event) is flirting with tar and feathers. No civic groups exist at all, let alone flourish. Hubble's is probably the only hardware store in the country that doesn't even *stock* paint (are you paying attention, Guinness?). Nor, for that matter, do any of the city's 40-odd groceries and drugstores bother themselves with soap, toothpaste, or, heaven forefend, deodorant.

The incredible thing, according to the emergency folks, is that everyone seems more than content, even determined, to keep things precisely as they are, and have been for 176 years. Indeed, the very suggestion of change has the visible effect of sending shudders and convulsive sweats through the seldom-emotional gentry, a situation perhaps best illustrated by the town's unusual resolve on being notified that it would, of all things, be included in the coming year's Guinness publication. Its proud claim of no accomplishments whatsoever had obviously struck some sort of responsive chord with

Artist's sketch:

## Lethargy Luxor Inn & Suites

**18,000 luxurious rooms!**

**(Palm trees by pool made of glamorous Fibroweave)**
**- No actual pool -**
**- Beautifully painted to *look* like a pool -**

***Come visit, won't you?***

the admittedly-flabbergasted Brits, whose legendary pursuit of *accomplishment* can be traced back to the inception of Knighthood.

Moving with uncharacteristic speed and accord, they hastily erected a giant clapboard statue (if a *prone* figure can properly be described as having been "erected"), and forthwith christened the gargantuan monstrosity, *The Statue of Lethargy.* Lest their attitudes be misconstrued by anyone, anywhere, the following message now graces the horizontal eyesore:

***Give us your dolts, your dregs,***
***Your slimy masses, every worthless cuss,***
***Your wretched outcasts with their whisky kegs,***
***Send these, the lurching drunk and foul to us***

In a related decision that has stunned even veteran Lethargy-watchers – adding insult to clapboard, so to speak – the city has since announced that these identical words also will adorn the façade of both the Greater Lethargy Convention Center and the 18,000-room Lethargy Luxor Inn & Suites, each scheduled for completion early next summer

# THE LITTLE-KNOWN AGONIES OF SQUIRMING BULL

C: 2011 – Dr. Ron Pataky ---- Custom-Ransom-Notes.com

**Mrs. Bull welcomes hubby home**

That the renowned Sioux chieftain Sitting Bull was a formidable foe would be denied by no one familiar with the brave exploits and cunning strategy he demonstrated time and again on the field of battle – and certainly not by the courageous men who fought under Custer, had any of them lived to experience the luxury of hindsight.

But bravery itself is a puzzling phenomenon in man, frequently less of a manifest *permanent* attribute than a curious sort of fleeting aberration that somehow finds altogether common individuals rising to author uncommon deeds of selflessness and heroism. Without question, the latter seems more typically the case.

Occasionally, however, history does recount deviant examples of men somehow "born to fight" – individuals in whom a savage streak is glaringly apparent to all around them. The so-called "Tunnel Rats" of the Vietnam conflict come to mind. It has been said of them that one had to be part psychopath and part animal to survive at all in the literal underworld that comprised their bizarre existence.

Nor will it surprise most that sociologists lay much of the cause for such anti-social extremes at the mottled doorstep of purely environmental factors. The gentlest dog, after all, if in enough pain, may well bite even his beloved master. Is it any less reasonable, then, that a human being who has experienced enough pain, mental *or* physical, might develop a spirit of meanness that would drive him eventually to baffling acts of savage violence?

Sitting Bull, by all accounts, was such a man – a fierce, even vicious warrior whose lot it would be to know and live with excruciating pain throughout his entire adult life.

Clearly, it is a story whose time has come.

The fact is that, as a result of a severe hemorrhoid affliction that began quite early in life, Sitting Bull never actually *sat* after the age of nineteen. Indeed, if first-hand accounts can be believed, from the time a jealous teen love rival snuck red pepper sauce into his ever-present posterior balm, the great Sioux chief rarely even *stood* in one place for very long!

(It was about this time, according to Sioux historian John Little Pony, that Sitting Bull (Taya Kuta) began to be called Taya *Squanta*, or "Squirming Bull." But only by *very* close friends, Little Pony adds pointedly).

Could such early misfortune have set in motion a tragic collision course that eventually would culminate in the disaster at Little Big Horn? So it would certainly seem.

Imagine for a moment the sheer agony the young warrior must have endured on being inducted into the elite Sioux brotherhood of *Silent Eaters.* (See Britannica, Vol. IX, p. 243). Here we have the excruciating picture of a young man, not even able to sit, participating in an initiation ceremony that would require each anxious candidate, as a test of his manhood, to squat bare-bottomed on an uncooperative porcupine during the entire dessert course, a many-flambéed affair lasting several hours. (Their name, incidentally, came from the fact that they also were required to consume literal mounds of dried and brittle prairie chips *without noise!).*

Small wonder that Sitting Bull was rather quickly becoming a very, very angry young man. In fact, it was only about thirty days after this searing experience that the name of Sitting Bull became dramatically known to the U. S. Army at the Battle of Killdeer Mountain. By this time, reports the Britannica, "he was definitely on the warpath." He was made head of the Sioux nation in 1867, by which time his reputation had spread far and wide. Indeed, the colorful expression, "madder'n a red-peppered injun" had become an idiomatic mainstay in folk jargon from the Chesapeake to the Dakotas.

When gold was discovered in the Black Hills in the mid-1870s, the second treaty of Fort Laramie was wantonly violated by the white man (as others had routinely been), and prospectors by the thousands began flocking to what had been the peaceful and private domain of the Sioux nation. This naturally annoyed the Sioux, with Sitting Bull himself irritated not so much over the gold and stolen land as over the fact that the cool mineral streams that had proven so therapeutic to his hind parts were not overrun with grizzled and foul-smelling panners of ore.

Is it surprising that less than six months later, on 25 June, 1876, General Custer and all of the men under his immediate command were annihilated at Little Big Horn? Is it coincidence that during these months Sitting Bull had suffered in raging silence without so much as a single, soothing sitz bath? These are the questions. The clear answer, most historians agree, is that scalding revenge was as inevitable as tomorrow morning.

Sitting Bull's own ignominious demise came about in 1890, ironically at the hands of his own people. Dragged from his bed as an "agitator," in December of that year, he was beaten to death by Indian police.

Initially, the great Sioux chief was buried at Fort Yates. Ten years later, however, his remains were moved to Mobridge, South Dakota, where a granite shaft was erected to commemorate the fact that he was finally entombed, according to his stated wishes, in a standing position.

The agony of the noble and long-suffering chief seemed finally behind him.

# THEY SIRED THE NIGHT DEPOSIT

**ROTHSCHILD!**, a mesmerizing new book by the eminent Vatican historian Fr. Anatoly Vichyssoise, reveals for the very first fascinating time the altogether humble origins of the fabled Rothschild family, whose matchless financial wizardry laid the foundation not only for banking as we know it today, but also for a dynastic fortune such as the world has seldom seen, before or since.

The earliest Rothschild of record, according to Fr. Anatoly's exhaustive research, was Bohemond "Bo-Bo" The First, an obscure 11th Century fisherman and toga-dyer from the small Italian village of Mafapunzo. It would become Bo-Bo Rothschild's fortunate lot one sweltering Mafapunzo afternoon to leave a modest herring catch inadvertently perched on a block of salt as he sloshed the final batch of an overdue chartreuse toga shipment he had been preparing for the Genoa Boy choir. (Salt, of course, was a much desired universal delight, colorfully described by children of the day as "the stuff that tastes bad when it isn't there").

In any event, it was a number of hours later when the usually conscientious Rothschild suddenly remembered the herring. Fearing the worst in light of the intense summer heat, he quickly dried his yellow-green hands and raced back to the salt block, where he was dumbfounded to discover his fish quite warm indeed, but nonetheless in a state of perfect preservation. The result of his brief memory lapse, as gourmands the world over well know, was the first-recorded incidence of salted herring, the thin strips of which quickly became a delicacy at the Vatican, where Urban II reigned as Pope.

Indeed, the dish was so relished by Vatican officials that Urban, mindful of the Crusades then on the drawing board, summoned senior aide Boris of Bouillon and instructed him to seek out the Mafapunzo toga-dyer forthwith. Specifically, the Pope desired to know if Rothschild might have any interest whatsoever in the proposed post of Official Caterer to the swelling legions about to plunder and otherwise lay waste to the Holy Lands, then occupied by heathen hordes.

Thus it was that Bo-Bo Rothschild catered the First Crusade; also that the ensuing Crusades, eight in all, were officially catered by ten successive Rothschild generations through 1291 A. D.

By that time, of course, establishment of a personal banking empire had become a clear matter of necessity, the family catering fortune having burgeoned to such an extent over a period of 196 years that no vault within several thousand miles came close to being large enough to house it. Indeed, the nearest adequate space was in the Asian province of Tanna Touva; it, however, was leased at the time to Mongol emperor Kublai Khan, and would not, as it turned out, become available until Khan's death three years later in 1294.

Frankfort was selected as the site of the first family bank because of its proximity to Offenbach, where Bo Rothschild X was involved in a serious dalliance with one Ophelia Gluck, daughter of a wealthy and prominent knockwurst baron. Branches followed soon thereafter in Vienna, London, Florence and Paris, as the Frankfort coffers almost immediately bulged at the seams, not only with coin of the realm and veritable wagonloads of sundry bank notes, but also with barrels by the thousands of surplus herring rendered more or less redundant when the last near-eastern stronghold of Akko fell to the Muslims.

Fr. Anatoly's book brims with spellbinding anecdotal material, not the least of which is the unsurprising discovery that the Rothschilds, from the first to the last, were centuries ahead of their time with regard to banking innovations.

Among other novelties, they were the first bankers anywhere to entice depositors with "premiums" (in 1299, a Londoner could get two "thoroughlie beeswaxe" candles for the deposit equivalent of 25 copper pennies). They also were the first to offer their patrons interest-bearing parchment deposits (PDs), and helpful hints on various other depository matters.

Probably the most innovative of their many contributions, however, were three absolute wowsers: their early implementation of an ingenious bank surveillance technique, the revolutionary "automatic teller," and ballpoint pens. Each in its way would drastically affect all future banking procedures. Each in its way carries over to this day as the standard of banks throughout the world.

***"Gezeigenhoftl!"*** ("absolutely astounding"), was the way one Frankfort police official described the Rothschild surveillance system, which employed a fast-scratching local "security sketcher" armed with a writing instrument and papyrus pad. As each male customer entered the bank (females were not permitted to touch money), the artist would hastily sketch his outstanding facial features, including what he was wearing at the time. When a rare bank heist did occur, the authorities were immediately provided with a solid likeness of the perpetrator, the usual result being that police were able to quickly track the culprit and actuate an arrest.

The automatic teller, on the other hand, was simplicity itself. Located in a cage within the bank's walls were two male persons - a small, bare-backed slave who could count without using his fingers, and a large guard wielding a short whip nastily studded with chipped seashells (known then as now in the industry as the chip-whip). The effect, of course, was that the inventive new teller's cage was swiftly rendered about as "automatic'" as such things get.

The ballpoint "pen" was simply unique; and, in fact, enabled both the security sketcher and the automatic teller to function in the first place. The Rothschilds began with a hollow quail quill, fitting the narrow end with a smooth sandstone pebble designed to absorb and retain liquid (which was squirted into the quill's larger open end). The liquid "inque" usually consisted of a dark berry stain of one variety or another. When coming into contact with papyrus, the obvious occurred: one could write and cipher with astonishing speed and accuracy. Moreover, it was conveniently portable

Observed one satisfied customer, who also happened to be a history buff: "Banking had not been nearly as practical when they relied on cuneiform."

The Rothschilds took the lead concerning many social issues as well, an example of which was a study on alcohol consumption, funded by the family and conducted during the early 14th century by the newly-founded but already prestigious Cambridge University. The result, after nine years of intensive research, was a huge volume entitled **"Dazed Knights: The Awesome Potency of Mead,"** in which the scholars concluded that the entire male population of King Arthur's Court undoubtedly, in their words, "frittered away the major part of their earthly existence in a condition best described as positively swacked."

The study went on to suggest that the legendary suits of armor (so romanticized in future stories and song) were probably "mere vestigial remnants of an earlier, infinitely more pristine era ...whose only redeeming trait was that they undoubtedly prevented many a fatality as besotted knights routinely toppled down long marble staircases or lurched from balconies high above cobblestone courtyards." (An occasion plunge into a moat, the study pointedly added, usually had precisely the opposite effect).

Still, and despite their undeniable philanthropy, the Rothschild family, as with the fabulously wealthy of all ages, took their share of flack from the masses. Among the many examples with which Fr. Anatoly regales us, for instance, is the fact that the entire original herring episode was to spawn a new adjective in coming centuries - the term "fishy" as it is now commonly used to describe the nefarious practices of bankers everywhere.

Also derived from the Rothschild's - and specifically from the outrageous rumors of "booty" that plagued the Rothschild's from year one of the very first Crusade - would come the now-classic Alice B. Toklas admonition, "Never ever trust a herring-scented toga-dyer."

# BACK WHEN THE OVAL OFFICE CARRIED WEIGHT

**President Willy as a child**

The day undoubtedly will come when presidential trivia supplies the minutiae desirable for the creation of some sort of adult parlor game. Such a game probably would be on store shelves now were it not for the fact that only 44 men presently qualify as subject matter. There are, after all, only so many facts one can milk from the personal and professional lives of but 44 men (or from 84, for that matter, which, come to think of it, pretty well takes us through the <u>next</u> two or three hundred years).

There's a second factor to consider as well. When the 44 (or 84) men all have served as President of the United States, facts concerning their fishbowl lives tend to fall into one of two categories: those reiterated with such redundancy by the American press that the average shiner of shoes is intimately acquainted with their most insignificant detail, or those so private and obscure to the public at large that no one short of a Washington bureau chief could possibly be aware of their shadowed existence.

Everyone, for example, knew of Ronald Reagan's voracity for jellybeans, perhaps even that his favorites were coconut and licorice. Lyndon Johnson's passion for bourbon and branch water was well documented, as was JFK's equally insatiable appetite for peccadilloes d'amour. Gerald Ford had played football at the University of Michigan. George Bush had been a very young and apparently capable pilot in World War II.

Less well known, but still pretty standard stuff, is the amusing fact of George Washington's wooden teeth. (Even less well known perhaps was the oft-cited cause of his having lost his teeth at such a young age...sugar-coated almonds of all things).

Andy Jackson's sweet-tooth disposition for blackberry jam (clearly reflecting his rural southern roots) might, come to think of it, be a nifty subject for an eventual parlor quiz. His response to a related question from a certain audacious reporter most certainly would be.

Asked which of the two he savored most, blackberry jam or Rachel, his doting wife of 37 years, the no-nonsense Jackson is said to have replied: "A good jam has more natural tang; on the other hand, she is not as seedy." (Jackson himself, as the first Democrat to occupy the White House, was considered by many to be seedy enough for them both!).

William Howard Taft may well represent the most fertile ground for such an eventual exercise in trivia. When his name does come up in cloakroom conversation (which admittedly is not all that often), most people, historians included, seem curiously vacant concerning the life (and appetites) of our 27th president. Even this, however, may be remedied with the release next year of a new, as-yet-untitled book by Taft biographer B. B. Peetelbloom.

For reasons which quickly become apparent, Peetelbloom devotes an inordinate amount of space to Taft's gargantuan appetite and somewhat non-specific preferences where food was concerned. As to Taft's favorite food, Peetalbloom merely chuckles. “Anything...anything at all," he says. "The man routinely would consume with shameless glee anything he could grasp in his sausage-like fingers, from a plump and veneered Christmas goose to a small caribou."

A classic example, according to the biographer, once involved a proposed visit by Taft to what was then Portuguese West Africa.

"It was to coincide with the famed gorilla roasts celebrated each year during the vernal equinox by the primitive Ibimbis," Peetelbloom relates. "The gorilla roasts were frolicsome week-long affairs during which a young gorilla female was lathered and shaved, then slowly rotated on a spit for seven days and nights until ready for the finger-licking culmination of the festivities.

"It became something of an embarrassment when Taft quite suddenly canceled the trip, explaining apologetically to the Portuguese land-lords that he had completely forgotten a prior engagement that would require his presence elsewhere.

"More than a few," says Peetelbloom, "suspected it had something to do with whispers around the White House to the effect that when a suitable gorilla female could not be located for one reason or another, the Ibimbis had a nasty habit of substituting an occasional tourist in her place. Taft, however, nervously laughed off such nonsense, insisting that the decision was based on the discovery that even very young gorillas consist of nothing but dark meat."

(In one of the more humorous asides, Peetelbloom relates

that the president, on being teased by cabinet member Pimbley Jeeters to the effect that Taft himself undoubtedly consisted almost exclusively of <u>white</u> meat, allegedly snapped back: "Oh, fiddle-your-dee-dee").

Trifling issues aside, however, the pertinent fact was that Taft's weight, as the result of an absolutely dissolute lack of anything resembling culinary discipline, exceeded that of Jackson, Ford, and Reagan combined. White <u>or</u> dark meat, of course, that was a substantial amount of flesh for a man who was not even a monarch; moreover, it would necessitate Taft's actually <u>doubling</u> the size of the White House west wing, which had been built by Teddy Roosevelt only seven years earlier.

Indeed, William Howard Taft, by virtue of his enormous size, had been the only presidential candidate in history to have exercised a little-known constitutional amendment permitting any individual of more than 350 pounds to run simultaneously on two tickets. Accordingly, as nominee of both the Progressive <u>and</u> Regressive parties during the scandal-ridden election of 1908, his campaign had the effect of pinning his middle-of-the-road opponent to the political center, so to speak.

In point of fact, his opponent that year, a Vermont congressman named Gwinnet Grimley, actually received more votes running on his popular "Centerstripe" platform than Taft himself received on either of his two individual tickets. Only the *combined* votes of both the Progressive and Regressive campaigns would eventually gain Taft the office of the Presidency (voters were, after all, voting for the same man).

Taft served only one term, almost reluctantly seeking re-nomination in 1912 against fellow Republican and former friend Teddy Roosevelt, with whom he'd had a minor falling out over the latter's constant use of the word "bully," which Taft considered "as annoying as a bootful of bees."

The Taft-Roosevelt rift served to split the Republican vote, enabling Woodrow Wilson to claim the White House for the Democrats. And therein lays a touch of irony.

Within weeks of the Democrat victory, it was discovered (to the delight of some and mortification of others) that Bertha Wilson, the new president's <u>wife</u>, outweighed both Taft and Roosevelt combined - indeed, by anywhere from 30 to 40 ounces, depending on the day's intake of pistachios and cherry vodka. Needless to say, it was a discovery that quickly became titillation in Washington social circles.

The campaign against Wilson was the last time Taft ever ran for public office (perhaps "chugged" would be a better choice of verbs), although he was appointed in 1921 as our 10th Chief Justice of the Supreme Court, serving in that capacity until just prior to his death in March of 1930. In retrospect, he is considered by historians to have been a superb jurist, a mild criticism being that the bench occasionally tended to be weighted in his favor. (That, and the single instance in which he uncharacteristically departed from protocol, casting an unprecedented three votes himself in the landmark New Jersey v. Apple Turnovers decision of 1928).

In declining health, Taft resigned as Chief Justice mere weeks before his death. He is our only chief executive, incidentally, to have died as the result of detonation, a tragic event that occurred when a well-meaning intern at St. Vincent's Hospital plunged what he perceived to be a life-saving syringe into the former president's bloated buttocks. Hundreds of windows were demolished, it is said, as far away as the White House, where even Herbert Hoover, the then-sitting president, was reported to have been nastily nicked on the neck by an indiscriminate flying shard.

Dressed in stately blue twill, hand-stitched on their own time by the good ladies of Bethesda Tent & Awning, Taft's body lay in state for three days in a converted diner car before being carried by

60 pallbearers (the hydraulic fork lift had not yet been marketed) to his final rest two miles distant in Arlington Cemetery.

Typically, there was a crude jokester in the crowd, in this instance a woman whose own figure was a tad short of svelte.

"Good thing he wasn't married to Bertha Wilson," she is said to have snidely sniffed. "They'd be the only husband and wife ever to maintain adjacent plots in different zip codes."

It was a remark most chose to mercifully ignore.

# THE PAINTER & THE PRESIDENT

**Only known photo of Fillmore without lectern**
**(Breaking ground with miniature shovel for new library)**

With the possible exception of Vincent Van Gogh, no artist of the past century-plus has been the subject of more literary conjecture than diminutive Henri de Toulouse-Lautrec, the French impressionist who's brief and tragic life has been the subject of no less than two dozen major books since his untimely death in 1901 at the age of only thirty-seven.

That he was an eccentric little fellow is indisputable; indeed, his long and curious association with an attractive Parisian dwarf lady named Fifi Olay has filled speculative volumes in itself. Still, according to Lautrec researcher Ephraim Fern, many – perhaps most – of the odd stories surrounding the artist's brief life appear to have been pure fabrication.

As an example, says Fern, no evidence whatsoever has surfaced to support the contention of numerous Lautrec buffs that the painter was so irrationally superstitious that he would routinely cross even the busiest street to avoid walking under a black cat. It is, according to the researcher, "simply an unfounded myth which unfortunately happens to coincide with the fact that Lautrec's death came as the result of being struck by a runaway milk wagon while crossing just such a street."

In point of fact, Fern claims, several witnesses have testified that there was not a single black cat within a three-square-block area at the time. "Best evidence," concludes Fern, "is that poor Toulouse was rather typically sloshed to the absolute gills that unhappy evening, and might just as easily have cart -wheeled down any of several embankments into the nearby Seine."

Not so incidentally, its seems somehow historically perverse that the average literate American probably knows significantly more about Lautrec than he or she does about Millard Fillmore, our 13$^{th}$ president and the last chief executive to represent the Whig political party – this despite the fact that the two historical giants shared so much in common.

We refer, of course, to their inordinately small physical stature.

Where Lautrec is concerned, the matter, as already noted, has always been common knowledge. For Fillmore, however, the fact of his incredible shortness (not unlike the later incapacitating illnesses of Wilson and Roosevelt) was virtually unknown outside of a small circle of close, personal friends, among whom even the Fillmore nickname, "Slats," was considered a matter of utmost discretion.

Where Lautrec's life and checkered career has provided history with a veritable mother-lode of compelling vignettes, no such mantle of intrigue surround the life of Fillmore, even though Fillmore's seventy-four total years exactly doubled Lautrec's age at the time of his death.

Still, and admittedly without data to support the probability, the extraordinarily short stature shared by the two men must have resulted in remarkable parallels in their respective lives, such being the usual experience of persons sharing a common physical trait.

Obviously, Fillmore was our shortest president by far, standing just over seventeen inches tall in his sandals. That his diminutive stature never became more generally known does seem an historical oddity, although certain disclosures concerning his own eccentricities help to explain how a secret of this minitude could have been so successfully kept throughout his lifetime.

There is but one recorded instance, for example – before, during, or after his presidency – of Fillmore ever having appeared in public without the presence in front of his body of a huge lectern of carved Rangoon teakwood. Indeed, residents of Upper New York State between the years of 1820-1874 were undoubtedly startled on occasion to witness what must have been the whimsical spectacle of their jolly neighbor navigating his familiar Popinjay Surrey from behind the very lectern that would accompany him throughout his life and career.

What was not known, of course, was that the bulky structure was specifically designed to mask the fact that behind it the tiny Fillmore invariably perched on a gigantic, hand-hewn cider cask, giving him the striking appearance of near-normal size. In later years, this innocent deception was enhanced by the additional fact that Fillmore never wore anything but vertically-striped suits when being filmed by early 1850s camera crews, thereby fooling the people by creating a celluloid illusion that made him appear more than four times his actual size in pre-Civil War newsreels. It was Millard Fillmore's grandson, Willard Fillmore, incidentally, who eventually would lose a tight state senate race in upper New York State after he was quoted as saying, "You can fool all of the people some of the time, and some of the people all of the time; but if you're *really* slick, you can generally hoodwink every last one of the stupid bastards!"

While Fillmore was generally seen in vertically-striped apparel, Lautrec, of course, never wore anything but black suits. It was a habit largely influenced by his long business alliance with the aforementioned Mademoiselle Olay, with whom he augmented his always-meager income by posing for bride and groom caricatures for the tops of wedding cakes.

One fact of their respective lives dramatically differentiated both the way that each lived his life, and the manner in which each would one day pass on to oblivion. Lautrec, it seems, suffered from a perpetual and utterly monumental thirst for anything alcoholic, with the dreaded absinthe being a singular favorite. Indeed, he often was seen wearing his familiar *"Mad for Wormwood"* tee-shirt in and around even the better gin-mills of the Champs de Elysses. Sadly, it was as the result of this unhappy proclivity that he met with so early and ignominious an end.

Fillmore, on the other hand, preferred lukewarm chamomile tea (jasmine, it is said, when feeling particularly festive), with an occasional oat biscuit thrown in on special occasions. He died peacefully in 1874 at age 74 -- because, some say, he considered it the right thing to do.

Millard Fillmore, incidentally, was our only president to have embraced the obscure *Hailakite* faith. As the unusual name suggests, the near-extinct sect, which traces its roots directly back to Valkyrie Valhalla, was originally founded on kite worship, believing as the cornerstone of its somewhat unorthodox theology that humans, when they die, get their souls get stuck in the branches of tall trees, from which it is all but impossible to get them back down.

# DENTURES: SHOULD YOU RENT OR OWN?

Say what you will about Dr. Winston ("Call me Winst") Phobe, the phenomenally successful "television dentist" from Secaucus, New Jersey: Like him or loathe him, the man has a definite flair for the limelight. Indeed, there are those who consider the 63-year-old dentist's knack for making headlines nothing short of unprecedented, particularly in light of the wildly diverse nature of his news-making forays.

Regular viewers of the ***First Friday*** television program will remember Phobe as the subject of a recent, highly complimentary segment in which interviewer Sherman Oachs highlighted the extraordinary response during the past year to television commercials promoting Dr. Phobe's nine-year-old denture rental chain, ***Bite 'N Chew, Inc.***

Dr. Phobe's novel notion to rent and/or lease dentures was, he says, predicated on his conviction that there are many people "out there" who simply cannot afford to buy them. His sales pitch, which resulted in more than 391 million dollars in rentals during the first six years of operation, is offered on more than 200 independent stations nationally – most, he good-naturedly admits, "those mom and pop outfits featuring old movies and *Leave It to Beaver* re-runs."

For a flat fee of $18 monthly, Dr. Phobe's patients either rent or lease their dentures "guaranteed to fit or your money back," with an option to purchase "only if completely satisfied" at the end of eighteen months. As Phobe convincingly reassures during the course of his persuasive commercials, "That's less than some folks spend on breath mints!"

Phobe is quick to emphasize that his purchase option "is just that - an option," adding, "even though every red cent can be applied to purchase at any time during the terms of the contract, it's frankly fine with me if patients choose to go on renting until their gums fall out."

As one might guess, Dr. Phobe's unique rental offer has resulted in its share of humorous situations. "You'd be amazed how many folks rent two sets just to have a spare around the house," he laughs. "That's one side of the coin."

The other, he says, are "more couples than you'd believe" who rent a single set between them. "Sort of time-sharing at its coziest," he chuckles, quickly adding, "You understand, of course, that cannot guarantee a fit if the teeth are being worn by more than one person."

The dentist recalls one time when a proper fit was academic. "We had a funeral home call us wanting to rent a set for a two-day showing … imagine."

Quite apart from his dental expertise and colorful (some say garish) salesmanship, Dr. Phobe also is highly regarded as an interpreter and uncanny prognosticator of seismic events. Indeed, he frequently is contacted from as far away as Buchistan and Tierra del Fuego by scientists seeking his analysis of one sort of subterranean rumble or another. Perhaps his most astounding seismological flair is his disconcerting genius for predicting with pinpoint accuracy a major earth disturbance weeks in advance of its onset; and, not infrequently, as distant as Madagascar and Abyssinia. Asked how he explains this truly unique forecasting ability, he smiles quizzically over his reading glasses. "I don't know, really. It's just something I sense in my teeth. Left molars might suggest Equatorial Africa, right bicuspids may favor the Pacific Rim, incisors could zero in on Vladivostok … that sort of thing."

His astounding prognostications notwithstanding, it was Phobe's recent discovery that New York City is moving westward at a rate of a quarter inch a year that has caused such a monumental upheaval in the world scientific community, becoming the cover story for no less than thirty-five major journals throughout the world, and making the covers of both ***Time*** and ***Newsweek.***

Typically, the dentist treats his newest discovery with equanimity. "Oh, it's a certainty, all right; but not really much of a concern for the immediate future," he comments reassuringly.

"Eventually, of course, the fact could be of some significance to New York companies for whom a corporate move seems in the offing. Down the road, so to speak, the city's gradual westward movement inevitably will affect any number of normal business expenditures – phone bills, for example.

"By the year five million and thirty-one, to give you an idea, New York to St. Louis will be a local call – St. Louis, you understand, is staying where it is. Moreover – talk about exciting projections! – *that* condition, once achieved, should remain more or less stable for durn near 71,000 years, providing, of course, there are no rate increases during that time."

Adds the dentist: "I'll naturally want to recheck my calculations; but then again, there's certainly no rush, is there?"

Winston Phobe, despite an outward air of easy calm, is without question a man on the move. His ***Bite 'N Chew*** projections for the coming year exceed $225 million in rentals alone ("and we have no idea whatsoever as to how many folks are going to *buy* their choppers"), and he continues to take up to six calls a day from scientists around the globe concerning actual or potential seismic occurrences.

"Most of them aren't much, really," he says modestly. "Some fuddy-duddy wanting to know if Mount What's-Its-Name is going to blow and louse up the monkey mating season or some such. It's actually quite rare to encounter anything genuinely exciting."

That's *his* view. Scientists throughout the world paint a quite different picture concerning the Secaucus dentist and his awesome gift for predicting the unpredictable. Virtually all call him genius. Many have taken to referring to him by one of his three unsolicited nicknames -- "BH" (for bloodhound), "Big Nose," or "Sherlock." Clearly, Winston Phobe is a man whose work has gained the respect and admiration of the finest scientific minds on the planet.

Almost incidentally, many will recall that Phobe's first real international exposure occurred when his were chosen the official dentures of the 1992 Olympic Games in Barcelona, Spain.

# THE DAY THE CANINES STRUCK

C: 2011 – Dr. Ron Pataky ----- Custom-Ransom-Notes.com

**WILFRED: AN INNOCENT BYSTANDER**

Contrary to common misperception, the Boxer Rebellion had nothing at all to do with Charlton Heston. As is so often the case when scuttlebutt and the passage of time join forces to reshape history (the rumors linking Lizzie Borden and the dairy company come to mind), the genesis of the bizarre "connection" between the Academy Award-winning actor and the historical event is fuzzy at best. Like bad habits, however, and despite overwhelming evidence to the contrary, myths have a way of persisting.

In point of fact, the incident involved a particularly disruptive labor strike in the summer of 1919 on the part of the canine residents of the world's largest Boxer breed kennel, located then as now in Moose Jaw, Saskatchewan, Canada. At issue, reports of the day indicate, were "feeding hours, tedious cuisine, general sanitation, and other grievances."

The strike erupted quite unexpectedly on an otherwise normal Wednesday morning in April. Before the walk-out was finally settled, six troublesome months would pass, during which time the once close-knit community of Moose Jaw would become appallingly divided over issues that seemed to grow uglier with each passing day.

One side loudly proclaimed that outside agitators were responsible for the fuss, pointing to the "sudden influx of New York types" as evidence of their divisive and hysterical accusations.

(In the less hysterical light of retrospection, it was discovered that only one New Yorker, a churn-maker from Oswego, had moved into the area during the entire episode; furthermore, that he was utterly dispassionate when it came to dogs).

The opposing side - technically the canines themselves, although represented by a battery of SPCA attorneys (<u>they</u> were from New York!) - charged among other things in their brief that sanitation was woefully inadequate and that the daily gruel on which the canines were forced to subsist was "not even of a quality fit for cats." (As the reader might reasonably surmise, Saskatchewan is emphatically <u>not</u> cat country).

After several months of bickering, arbitration seemed the only possible answer to the tenacious deadlock. Local Mounties, having declared a state of emergency, called upon the venerable Royal Canadian Canine Board to mediate the mess. Even this proved fruitless after several weeks, however, and tension in the small community continued to mount.

Threats of violence, virtually unheard of in the friendly community up until that time, became commonplace, and a particularly naive view was taken by many concerning the altogether normal behavior of certain Boxer males accused of crossing imaginary "picket lines" to visit and otherwise cavort with attractive females on the other side.

At the end of four full months, the situation had taken on an air of hopelessness. Neither side seemed willing to give an inch, and saturnine grumblings continued to spoil many an otherwise sunny day, not to mention close friendships of long-standing. One local resident, a crop-duster named Mackenzie Furlong, summed up the feelings of the area's numerous unaffiliated, commenting simply, "Sad day, ey?" It was, in the colorful vernacular of the region, a mouthful.

Also marring reality were dire predictions of possible future ramifications based on the present precedent. Included among these were the crackerbrained notions of one local eccentric who, in typically dotty fashion, commented that, "this sort of strike mentality is someday gonna spread to professional athletes and public servants, jist wait an' see!"

He, of course, was ignored by both sides.

Just when it seemed that things could not possibly get worse, the inevitable Law of the mischievous Murphy descended like a plague on Moose Jaw. First, the town reservoir, source of the area's entire water supply, was found to be contaminated with (of all things) Blue Heron droppings. Moose Jaw, already fuming over the continuing Boxer Rebellion, suddenly found itself without drinking water.

It was at this precarious point that the local brewery, deserted for want of potable water, caught fire, burning to a flat raven crisp quicker than the local volunteers could say barley and hops.

To say that both sides were thoroughly disheartened would have been considerably understating the case at that sorry moment in time. Somehow, with decent water unavailable and the town brewery gone, the will to carry on the fight rather quickly evaporated. Predictably perhaps, the plight of a few recalcitrant dogs came into saner perspective and an earlier suggested solution, thought too radical by many at the time, was immediately implemented.

Within 24 hours, local officials, acting with an accord that resembled impetuosity, had imported 50 Pit Bull Terriers of exceptionally bad temperament from an illegal breeder in the Wisconsin dells. Within 45 minutes following their sullen arrival in Moose Jaw, violence had subsided completely and the disastrous six-month insurrection was summarily quelled. Within a week, the reservoir had been thoroughly disinfected, within a month the brewery rebuilt from scratch. Moose Jaw, bruised and only ever so slightly bowed, quickly returned to normal.

Such it was, subsequent fictional reports and/or motion pictures notwithstanding, that the true chronicle of the Boxer Rebellion finally came to its idyllic conclusion. The happy resolution of the nasty business found former long-time friends gratefully renewing their friendships, a goodly number of families ecstatically reunited, and even the dogs once again seemingly content to loll in the long shadows of autumnal sunlight, their pink tongues hanging humorously from the sides of their mouths in delicious anticipation of the first invigorating evening frosts in scenic Saskatchewan. It was, to be certain, a storybook ending.

Pit Bulls, incidentally, gain their name from the fact that their sole diet consists of cherry, peach, and apricot pits, the resulting constipation from which makes their eyes squint.

# Ferunzo Amapoli: RENAISSANCE MAN

Even in the small Neapolitan suburb in which he has lived for all of his 37 years, the name of Ferunzo Amapoli is virtually unknown to the average man on the street (described for our purposes here as approximately 5' 9", weighing about 155 pounds, with dark brown to black hair, and some with moles on their right cheeks. At least one has a retained "Viva il Duce" tattoo above his left navel. These statistics represent the official average man on the street for the area in question).

Like many of us, Amapoli is recognized on sight by any number of people in the immediate neighborhood; but even these, for the most part, know him by face rather than by name. Ironically, even the local postman has greeted him each morning for years as Signor Funiculino, which, as it turns out, is the name of his absentee landlord, a retired forger of government documents who presently (as of 2010) makes his comfortable home in Stuttgart.

So, what is so unusual about this particular example of otherwise typical urban anonymity? Nothing really, except for the utterly astounding fact that Amapoli is generally considered to be among the five top physicists *and* economists in the entire world! That, as Will Rogers might have said, is a powerful packet of credentials to be borne along by such an unassuming young fellow -- which Ferunzo most assuredly is.

Amapoli's theoretical work in both physics and economics has indeed left an indelible mark on the world scientific community, where one might reasonably expect him to be something more than merely another face in the crowd. But the scientific community has a kind of anonymity all of its own. There, via the worldwide net, television, and professional journals throughout the globe, his name is well-known to all. And still almost no one would recognize him on sight if he strolled up one day and began nibbling their prize begonias. (The scientific community, you may have noticed, is almost the exact opposite of the normal suburban community).

Is it an unfortunate situation that nags at the undeniable genius? Au contraire, he would cheerfully reply, happily pointing out that he has the absolute best of both worlds -- fortune and name-fame, but with a privacy and freedom of movement that kings, dictators, and presidents would kill for (and have!).

Where the scientific community is concerned, Amapoli is never content merely with disproving or confirming an axiom or theory. As with most of his experimentation, scientific result is his primary objective to be sure; but Ferunzo, ah dear Ferunzo ... HE has something else! Second only to his diligent search for demonstrable truth at all times and in all things is his boisterous flair for the flamboyant teaching of it, his theory being that entertaining, even comical touches are one way young people can be willingly drawn, (indeed almost unknowingly!), into the otherwise ominous arena of physics, mathematics, and the like.

It was the small and unassuming Neapolitan, for instance, who most recently verified Galileo's original experiment concerning what effect the weight of an object has on the speed with which it falls from a given height. To make his point, he journeyed from his southern home to the northern Italian city of Viareggio, where the nearby and well-known Leaning Cliffs of Carrara provide precisely the overhang required for re-verification of the classic Galileo experiment.

To the delight of local youngsters, most of them drawn to the site by a newspaper article of the day before, Amapoli corroborated Galileo's earlier findings in his usual flashy fashion, demonstrating to the youthful, wide-eyed assemblage the following: If you drop a single gigantic watermelon and an entire wagonload of cantaloupes from exactly the same height at precisely the same moment, they will both reach the ground a mere fraction of a second before an incredible, all consuming mess. The youngsters, of course, were delighted by the splashy demonstration. (Carrara sanitation workers were, perhaps expectedly, somewhat less enthralled).

As mentioned earlier, Amapoli's skill as a physicist routinely has been matched by his unparalleled knack for simplifying the extraordinarily complex. It was, for example, this Wizard-like gift (in this instance as an economist) that finally reduced the prodigiously elaborate concept of Gross National Product (GNP) to a level which even some elected leaders are almost able to comprehend.

To more clearly illustrate his point, Amapoli selected as his example the GNP of the small principality of Andorra, located in the Pyrenees and home of the giant dog breed of the same name.

Although a modest GNP such as Andorra's makes it easier for the average mind to conceptualize (yes, even including the generally under-average minds of elected leaders on occasion), Amapoli insists that the GNP of any nation, however large, can be ascertained by using his same basic one-size-fits-all formula, to wit:

"The GNP of any nation can be accurately determined at any given moment by quartering its total and multiplying your finding by a factor of eight, then dividing the result by two." The actual concluding GNP figure, he says, naturally changes from year to year, but the same formula remains applicable whenever and throughout.

Even in the ultra-cautious and super-competitive world of science, where jealousy and backbiting are traditionally rampant, Amapoli's simple equation has met with universal acclaim, its validity unchallenged by even the most mulish among his peers.

Interesting enough, the rarified arena of scientific and economic research nearly lost Amapoli to a career in royalty earlier in his youth. As some youngsters dream of becoming actors, singers, presidents, business tycoons, or major sports stars, young Ferunzo, from the time he was six or seven, had wanted to be a monarch. It was only the continual harping of his sainted, white-haired mother that eventually diverted the little fellow from the dubious goal he had set for himself so early in life.

"Royalty attracts the wrong sort," she would drum into his head day after day. "Look at those kids of Prince what's-his-name," she would hammer away. "Not one of them is worth the garlic it would take to baste them!"

The clear wisdom of her motherly leading eventually got through to the starry-eyed Ferunzo, and by the time of his nineteenth birthday, he had completely forsaken earlier visions of thrones and crowns for the scientific calling that has served him so well since. ("Thrones and crowns," he laughs today, "gave way to thorns and gowns").

Now, at age 37, Amapoli is revered by those who look upon him as something of a combined wit and spontaneous philosophical sage. Indeed, classic examples of his wry and penetrating humor were witnessed by many during his recent three-week American visit, his fourth in as many years. (Chortled one octogenarian in response to one of the droll and entertaining town-meetings hosted by the personable Amapoli: "I swear, there's more than a little Will Rogers in that boy!").

Touring southern Indiana after a speech he had given in Indianapolis concerning the continuing pressures brought to bear on the United States by the clover-producing nations of the Pampas, he more or less reached his comedic peak. After seven grueling hours of viewing what must have seemed to him endless Indiana pastures, streams, small hills, and valleys, the “Napoli Kid” (as he was dubbed by the American press) sat quietly over coffee at day's end with his American hosts. The subject had by then turned to oil and the Middle East.

Gazing thoughtfully out of a picture window at nature's rapturous handiwork in the form of an absolutely spectacular sunset, Ferunzo pondered the pastoral scene and thoughtfully reflected aloud, "Wouldn't it be glorious to wake up one morning and find that all of the Arab nations were in sudden and desperate need of dandelions?"

To his followers, reading of the remark in papers of the following day, it was pure, vintage Amapoli. Only the government of Yemen took exception, with a high-level Yemeni spokesperson quoted in the international press as having retorted, “Ha, ha, ha. The damned Napoli doofusnik probably thinks his poopers don’t stink! Come to Yemen, Wise Elegant One, and we will show you just how clouds and petrified artichokes are made!” (ED. NOTE: This translation has been questioned by the editors. Yemeni officials, however, had not returned their calls as of this writing).

# AN ASTONISHING HUE IS HALLOWEEN BLUE



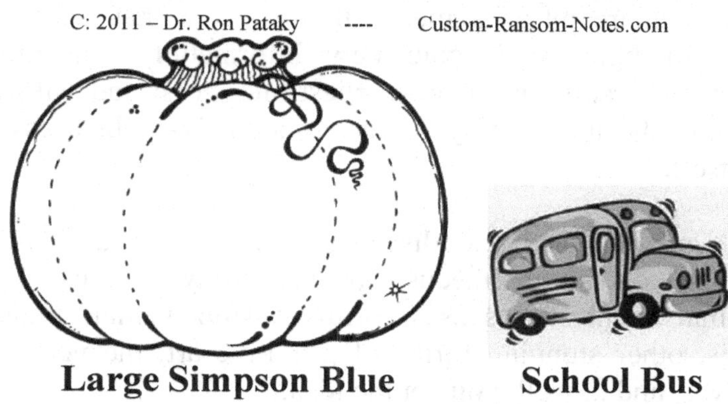

**Large Simpson Blue** **School Bus**

Ours is a world necessarily obsessed with the faithful and wondrous rhythms of nature - of the seasons themselves, of days that grow longer and shorter accordingly, of lunar phases and ocean tides, of hay fever and hurricanes, of blizzards and droughts, of heat-exhaustion and air-conditioning, of frostbite and antifreeze, of noisy nights and still waters, of ptomaine and Tabasco.

Less manifest, perhaps, but equally familiar on a more or less regional basis (less so with the advent of worldwide television), are such geographical specifics as the marvelous migrations resulting in the resolute return at the same time each spring of the swallows to Capistrano, and the legendary buzzards (actually turkey vultures) to the small community of Hinckley, Ohio.

Here in the United States, maple syrup and tulip bulbs are prominent in the spring, tomatoes and sweet corn by mid-summer, chestnuts and bock beer in the fall. Thyme, mint, chives, and oregano are perennial, parsley biennial. Basil, dill, and rosemary, alas, must in most climes be negotiated anew with the arrival each March of the regenerative vernal equinox. Certain locusts appear every seven years; others (cicadas) every 13 or 17, depending on the species. Halley's Comet, not to be outdone, comes our way but once every 76 years. And so it goes.

Present-day archeology, utilizing technology and translative techniques undreamt-of a mere 50 years ago, has succeeded in bringing to light remarkable new information concerning the lifestyles and traditions of our earliest ancestors; and with it, new insight into the inextricably-woven, steadfastly-cyclical essence of nature itself.

Many of the new discoveries were and are supremely glamorous - Australopithecus, majestic Mayan ruins, Egyptian tombs that numb the senses, brilliant Hopewellian tools, cave paintings, other stunning forms of primitive art, the very heavens themselves, and ... well, you get the idea.

Literally thousands of other examples admittedly are less well known, although their lack of archeological charisma in no way detracts from the data provided and awe engendered by their dynamic presence in the perfect overall scheme of things. In short, no "find," however obscure or insignificant it may seem, is by any stretch of the imagination irrelevant. Sooner or later, even the smallest piece fits surpassingly into nature's exquisite handiwork.

Among our finest examples of such little-known but utterly-fascinating finds is the exceedingly long-germinating Simpson Blue Pumpkin, whose existence was discovered a mere dozen years ago to the delight and astonishment of researchers in the relatively new field of artifact botany.

The Simpson Blue (as it is called) germinates but once every 313 to 319 years (depending on unseen ozone glissades and other global variables), and is, according to Stanford University's own Dr. Clinton Cluxstutter, due to blossom and eventually produce its gourd-like azure fruit some 20-26 years after the turn of the millennium, initially appearing as marble-like baubles on long, sinewy vines in the early spring of the year in question, and bursting full-forth by late September.

Says Dr. Cluxstutter: "We have known for centuries of the existence of a curious gourd-like blue fruit; moreover, that it clearly has thrived for millennia in virtually every corner of the globe. We find mention of it, for example, in the writings and-or art of an amazing collection of peoples, from the Babylonians and their chiselings to ancient Sanskrit, from early Aztec scratchings to the naughty Etruscans, from the Vikings to prehistoric pygmies and mammoth cave-dwellers.

"But it was not until two wonderfully-preserved specimens were discovered in a Magdalenian grotto by Doctor Waldo Simpson about 12 years ago that we were actually able to see first-hand the resplendent blue beasts, albeit petrified to veritable bowling balls. At first, in fact, Simpson actually thought he <u>had</u> come upon some sort of ancient bowling ball; on closer examination, however, his botanist companion would convince him otherwise."

Continues Cluxstutter: "The fact that the Blue Simpson germinates only once every 313 to 319 years is indisputable. Indeed, we find truly uncanny mention of it throughout literature, but <u>only</u> at precise 313 to 319 year intervals. The Simpson is never mentioned otherwise, not even in passing.

"In 1685, for example, John Alden recorded that he and the petite Priscilla were served 'blueish pumkind' (sic) at a reunion hosted by friendly Indians that fall in Duxbury, Massachusetts, in honor of the three remaining Mayflower survivors. Alden himself would perish there only two years later, the last of the male survivors.

"Before that," Cluxstutter goes on, "we find it mentioned in any number of Italian Renaissance writings during the early 1370s, and, of course, by the great-great-great grandson of Frankish King Charles the Simple in 1059. ("Simple" in this case meant something on the order of "common man," and not, as one might otherwise think, some sort of dolt whose voltage gauge was permanently stuck on Oafish).

"Even earlier, towards the end of the eighth century, mention was found among the childhood memoirs of Charlemagne himself. Then there was Valentinian III, the fifth-century 'poet-emperor' of Rome, who referred to 'the savory punkin of blue' in his classic epic, Ibid, which he completed in 433; and, of course, we should not overlook Pope Sixtus the First, who, in his papal bull of the year 120, made reference to 'his magnificent blue gourds' in describing a patron's meticulously manicured Roman garden.

"The simple fact," says Cluxstutter, "is that we have just this sort of conclusive record of the Simpson Blue dating about as far back as one can imagine. We know they had them in Ur of the Chaldees. They grew them along the banks of the Euphrates. Yes, and at the headwaters of the Yangtze, the Amazon, the Upper Volta, and the Nile as well. Certain cannibal tribes mashed them into a tasty basting paste...the Franks, the Druids, the Mongols...and, well, once again you get the idea.

"One very early account even had Cain slaying Abel in a fit of jealousy over the latter's larger and altogether superior stock of the "luscious mellow blue melons" (Abel, after all, was the farmer in the family). And who among us, after all, can say for certain? Sinners that we are, maybe the Simpson Blue was actually the forbidden fruit!

"Whatever the case, however," he continues, "it is absolutely vital, once again, to remember that they are never, never mentioned in literature other than at definite 313 to 319 year intervals. Never once! Not even a single lousy mention! Nada! Nyet! None!"

Needless to say, artifact botanists are anxiously awaiting the moment only a few years hence when modern man will have his first glimpse (and taste!) of the legendary Simpson Blue.

"After all," Cluxstutter reminds one and all, "we won't have another crack at that baby until at least the year 2314, plus or minus, when someone, perhaps having read ours or the literature of others, will be as eager as we are now for the big moment to finally flower on the scene.

"Just imagine," he says with a disbelieving chuckle, "Blue pumpkin pie."

An additional plus, says the scientist, may be that the Simpson Blue will be discovered to have some sort of medicinal value. Perhaps even a profound one.

"Of course, we are being cautious about this," he says, "...and frankly we're not all that optimistic. Still, there is some indication, based on one tattered set of barely legible documents recently found in an ancient Nepalese dungeon and carbon-dated at about the seventh century B. C., that silent monks (at least we call them monks; and we don't think they talked) once utilized a 'blue ball salve' - almost certainly a reference to the Simpson Blue - in the treatment of warts, boils, 'the itch,' shingles, and scabies. It's all quite sketchy, of course, mentioned only that single time in all the writings through the centuries. Actually, however, the paucity of reference is not all that surprising. The medicinal urgency of anything available only every 300 or so years is, after all, minimal at best.

"Let's face it," he concludes with a hearty laugh, "if you missed getting your prescription filled during the precise year-or-so in question...well, let's just say that the pharmacy didn't open again for a long, long time."

Cluxstutter, by the way, also is extremely excited about a new variety of mint recently unearthed in excavations near Carbondale, Illinois, where the Freudian Indians once lived. The diggers there, for what turns out to be the obvious reason, call it Hot Pink Mint.

"It is hot pink, indeed!" exclaims Cluxstutter. "Can you imagine anything smelling that good looking that good?! And could it just possibly be that this was the source of the hot pink craze that hit the Freudians like an anvil thump about A. D. 600 or 700? I tell you, old Von Poopsie in Vienna would have jumped on this like a horned toad on a fat gnat." (See earlier accompanying post: Freudian Slips and Other Undergarments).

"I swear," the scientist exclaims with finger-snapping, thumb-sucking glee, "it just never ends, does it? It just doesn't end at all!"

(We probably should mention in passing that Rutherford B. Hayes was the first American president to own a telephone. Since he was the only person in Washington with a telephone, it kind of makes one wonder what possible purpose the thing served. It reminds one somewhat of the north Chicago high-rise owner who purchased an elevator that only went in one direction. At least the Chicago fellow got to use his toy once! But perhaps I digress...).

**Hot Pink Mint**
**(In full bloom)**
**YUM!**

# HE WHO SO SHALL SO THEN SHALL HE WHO

C: 2011 – Dr. Ron Pataky ---- Custom-Ransom-Notes.com

Depending on one's view of the British in general, and depending on the level of one's contempt for 19th century British philosophy in particular, documents found in his private files following the death this past spring of England's controversial Lord Wickershaft, Third Earl of Buttonshire, are certain to elicit strong responses one way or another.

For resolute Anglophobes, reaction more than likely will be one of haughty disdain, perceived as mere confirmation of their long-held belief that the British are a pompous and arrogant race whose usefulness on the planet has been in serious doubt since shortly after Stonehenge (a rare exception, most agree, being Shakespeare).

Those whose primary contempt is reserved for British *Philosophy*, on the other hand -- "If walls could talk, we could have a nice chat," and *that* sort of thing -- are more likely to simply shake their heads at what they consider merely another example of the obdurate tendency on the part of British philosophers to ignore anything resembling actual wisdom in favor of continued fawning at the altar of insignificance.

For persons clinging to the latter belief, the Wickershaft collection provides a veritable mother lode of useful ammunition.

Consider, for example, the banal and heretofore unknown "Avoidance Theory," postulated in 1819 by Sir Farfel Grunion, then executive director of the Royal Pharmacological Society, and considered one of England's most prominent amateur philosophers (assuming, of course, that such a thing as a *professional* philosopher exists; at best, critics respond, these persons are self-appointed and quite often warped).

The substance of Grunion's hypothesis after nearly half a century's work is summed up in the final sentence of his 847-page treatise, completed in 1825 and titled *The Void in Avoidance.* "An ounce of prevention," Sir Farfel concluded, "is found to have been one-sixteenth of a pound."

Needless to say, for those capable of following the complexities of his logic, he did have a point. Detractors, however, made their point as well, perhaps most succinctly summed up by one Greevy Botsworth, a Liverpool net-mender and occasional scholar, who in 1827 posed the intriguing question, "SO?!"

(Sir Farfel, incidentally, was the same gritty fellow who elected to tackle head-on no less a philosophical giant than Descartes himself, disputing the latter's renowned "Cogito Ergo Sum" on the basis that it should have been, in Grunion's words, "I *say* so, therefore I am; For if I were not, I could not say so; although even being, I am free to claim I am not, although I don't." In the wake of his pronouncement, many wondered, why?).

But enough of Farfel Grunion. As clearly reflected in the Wickershaft collection, 19th century Britain spawned far, far too many succulent examples to dwell on but one.

British Viscount (and amateur philosopher) Sir Philip Audubon, cousin of the French naval officer Jean Audubon, whose dalliance in 1774 with a lady in Haiti resulted in the birth of the famed naturalist and bird-painter John James Audubon, is a case in point.

To the chagrin of the artist Audubon and his British co-author William MacGillivray (*Ornithological Biography,* 5 vol., octavo, 1831-39), the Viscount cavalierly dismissed the wondrous paintings *and* research of his talented second-cousin as "flapdoodle," concluding a lengthy thesis on the subject with the obvious observation that a bird in the hand "is simply messy."

Still another example from the Wickershaft files involved Fr. Alistair Dunk, a Druid priest and maternal grandfather of American naturalist Luther Burbank. Clearly not a man who comprehended the "big picture" (as his grandson would later prove to be), the elder Dunk (Luther's mother's father) observed in 1803 -- to the astonishment of almost no one - that "Little acorns from mighty oak trees fall." Needless to say, his solemn pronouncement produced barely a ripple in the clouded stream of philosophical progress.

Some ripples, however, have been pronounced.

"Classic balderdash" is the way one critic has described the recently discovered "minutes" of the Royal Conjectural Society's annual meeting in 1849, in which Sir Ramsgate Pheester suggests to his long-time crony, Sir Henry Tweet, the following: "Being unable to reach a conclusion as to which of the two evils, procrastination or indecision, we find least admirable, we very probably should table the question indefinitely."

One matter they did not table, however, was putting their official stamp of approval on Sir Ramsgate's proposed theorem: "Any object is precisely two times as long as the distance from its precise middle to either end." It, according to the minutes of the meeting, was passed unanimously by voice vote, "with nary a nay."

(The minutes, incidentally, also include a humorous footnote. At one point during the meeting, "a browne skin type," apparently a self-styled guru of some sort, burst into the chambers, leapt upon a table, and sent the assemblage into near-cardiac arrest by screaming, "To be or not to be; that is the *answer!*" An immediate recess was called.).

Close examination of the Wickershaft papers, however, clearly demonstrates that all was not necessarily poppycock. As with even the dullest of eras, *some* intelligent life seems to have been extant during the blighted period, undoubtedly residue of the Renaissance. Still, the collection is monumentally weighted on the side of the sublimely fatuous.

There are some delightful exceptions: Philosopher Finley Pipple's revision of an old 17th century children's chant seems a thoroughly delightful illustration of what some have called the "nearer my truth to thee" syndrome. Wrote Pipple in 1853: "Sticks and stone may break my bones; but *names* really piss me off!" Pipple's observation was followed closely thereafter, in September of the same year, by his Cousin Millard Priddle's equally well-known *obiter dictum,* "There's a little bit of ourselves in each of us." Priddle, incidentally, was the Shoreham sonnet-writer who departed from his chosen field to write the following concerning one of Britain's most renowned heroes:

***His name is known throughout the world***
***A man of saintly spheres***
***His, a world of dreams unfurled***
***Through many times and years***

***A vapor-ring of confidence***
***Shown 'round him like an arch***
***His wisdom helped to make some sense***
***Of life with too much starch***

***"THE HUSH OF LIFE IS WRAPPED IN HUGS"***
***(The quote that brought him fame)***
***And that is how ENAMEL GLUGS***
***Became a household name!***

Another 19th century drollery that quickly gained public favor was a variation on an earlier observation by Sir Walter Scott, penned in 1864 by Lord Leighton Cranberry, then Chief Physician to the Court of St. James. Concerned regarding what he described as "the malady of the fledgling physician," Cranberry observed: "O, what a tangled web we weave, when at first we practice."

(Lord Leighton, incidentally, is not to be confused with the esteemed mathematician Dr. L. *Layton* Cranberry, whose classic work, "Five Simple Methods for Measuring a Yardstick," remains, nearly two centuries after its writing, the definitive work on the subject).

The final word, however, seems to have been had by a passionate philosophobe named Thelonius Anonymous, who included among his prodigious collection of poems, short stories, and general observations any number of barbed references to philosophers and their (to him) questionable product.

One Rabelaisian observation in particular, which Anonymous called *Poetic Justification,* certainly summed it up for many. Wrote Anonymous:

***Regarding the legend***
***Of early birds***
***And the bilge we've all been taught***

***The early bird***
***Gets the worm all right***
***But the early WORM gets caught!***

Argue with that if you can…

# Behold Benediction

Regarding what you've read herein
You mustn't be too shaken
Unless of course you bought this book
In which case you've been taken

The Management